HILDA DAVID is an Associate Professor of English at the Symbiosis College of Arts and Commerce in Pune. A novelist, stage director and teacher, she also coordinates the Centre for Liberal Arts, where she teaches Advanced Creative Writing.

FRANCIS JARMAN taught English, Cultural Studies, and Intercultural Communication at Hildesheim University, Germany, until his retirement in 2013. Dr. Jarman has also taught or lectured in Egypt, Thailand and Japan, and at 18 European universities, and been a Scholar-in-Residence at Symbiosis, Pune, and a Visiting Professor at American College, Madurai. He is a novelist, critic, playwright and a classical numismatist.

INDIA DIVERSITY

Edited by

Hilda David
Francis Jarman

Om Books International

First published in 2017 by

Om Books International

Corporate & Editorial Office
A-12, Sector 64, Noida 201 301
Uttar Pradesh, India
Phone: +91 120 477 4100
Email: editorial@ombooks.com
Website: www.ombooksinternational.com

Sales Office
107, Ansari Road, Darya Ganj,
New Delhi 110 002, India
Phone: +91 11 4000 9000
Fax: +91 11 2327 8091
Email: sales@ombooks.com
Website: www.ombooks.com

ISBN: 978-93-86316-97-4

Printed in India

10 9 8 7 6 5 4 3 2 1

CONTENTS

Foreword

Hilda David

Dr. Hilda David is an Associate Professor of English at the Symbiosis College of Arts and Commerce in Pune. A novelist, stage director and teacher, she also coordinates the Centre for Liberal Arts, where she teaches Advanced Creative Writing. She has been a consultant to the Norwegian Ministry of Foreign Affairs, and coordinated and organised the Ibsen Festivals in Pune and Delhi. She was chosen by the English Speaking Union to represent India at the Shakespeare Workshop in London in 2008. Her works have been translated into Hindi, Urdu and Kannada.

This book is a cry against the same old, same old. Or the opportunism pushed by publicists and their agents.

When I first met Francis Jarman in 2010, we spoke about why deploying our imaginations, and providing for others to use theirs, is an obligation for all citizens. This book is his child. And it testifies to his range of interests, and a commitment to the cause.

First, a bit of a flashback.

When I attended the Sawai Gandharva Bhimsen Mahotsav (as it is christened now) at the New English School Raman Baug grounds in Pune, I knew when to nod at a *samm* (the first beat of a rhythmic pattern) or *taal* (rhythm). I was not trained. So, I can say, it was ingrained in me. Many questions popped up in my head. Is it because of the *mehfils* (private performances of music or poetry) and *sangeet nataka* (musical dramas) in Miraj? (I was seated (and later, dozed off) on the lap of my doctor father.) Could it be traced to Sawai Gandharva's birth-place in Kundgol in Karnataka in the 19th century? Or could it be located to the *riyaz* (music practice) sessions with Sawai Gandharva's guru, Ustad Abdul Karim Khan? Or an *azaan* (call to prayer) from a nearby mosque or a hymn in the church (which, I must confess, I rarely visit)? Or watching in awe, when common folk utter the words of the *bhakti* (devotional) saints, en route from Dehu to Pandharpur?

These are the things which have been the cornerstone of my life. When in doubt, I return to these things.

In a way, this compilation celebrates the same spirit.

The importance of the essays in this book can be understood because of the breadth of the contributions.

It can be celebrated through the poems by Sanjukta Dasgupta and Peer Khan, Meena Kandasamy and Arundhathi Subramaniam.

Or in the dialectics of Armene Modi ("Voices for the Voiceless—Transforming Women's Lives in Rural India"); or in the gritty provocativeness with which Ramu Ramanathan spoke to our students about the cruelty of governments ("Voices of Dissent in Maharashtra").

There is filmmaker Rakesh Sharma's bleak but sizzling political analysis ("After the Election—What Next?"); and the pugnacious and brave M.H. Zaffar ("Religious Fundamentalism and Secularism—With Special Reference to Islam").

There are the poets R. Raj Rao ("Gay in India?") and Dibyajyoti Sarma ("Cultural Diversity in the North East of India"), who re-oriented my cultural horizons with brimming and tartly phrased political sensibility. And then there are the mythologies of Jerry Pinto ("The Shared Space of Bollywood" and "Scenes from a Life in Diversity") and Arshia Sattar ("Diversity within the Valmiki Ramayana"); and Joel Timothy's "Church in the Liminal Space—Limitations and Possibilities".

There is a lot more that is candid, informal, alert, learned, tongue in cheek, but, above all, a cry for human dignity.

I sincerely hope that you enjoy reading this special collection as much as I enjoyed watching it unfold, the texts being scoured and revised. Thanks are due to the contributors, but also to many others who gave their help or support, including Dr. Hrishikesh Soman, Dr. Sunayini Parchure, Ms. Jasmina Desai, Ms. Tessy Thadathil, Puja and Joshi Kaka. Special thanks go to Jerry Pinto, to Suhail Mathur, our literary agent of The Book Bakers, and to Dipa Chaudhuri, our editor at Om Books International.

If we have missed anyone, we beg their forgiveness; similarly, although we have made every effort to acknowledge the sources of contributions and quotations, if we have overlooked or got anything wrong, we will do our best to put it right in future editions of the book.

The individual contributions represent the views of their authors, of course, which are not necessarily shared by the editors or by the other contributors. But it would be fair to say that there is one view that is probably shared by everyone involved in this project: the conviction that this question of diversity is of huge importance to India today.

I began with music and so let me conclude with music.

A decade ago, on a nippy winter morning when I watched the legendary Bhimsen Joshi render a *taan* (a virtuoso vocal technique), I realised that this was his tribute to a raga named after a town linked in Hindu mythology to Lord Krishna, but the phrases were in praise of a 12th-century Sufi saint, Khwaja Moinuddin Chisti, the saviour of the poorest of the poor.

To imagine that a school boy grasped this, as he stood next to a shop in Gadag which sold gramophone records, and developed his music aesthetics based on what an illiterate shopkeeper played for future customers.

For me, that is diversity. And every single word in this book helps to create something that would justify that.

Happy Reading!

Pune, September 2016

INTRODUCTION: DIVERSITY AND ALTERITY

Francis Jarman

Dr. Francis Jarman taught English and Intercultural Communication at Hildesheim University, Germany, until his retirement in 2013. He has also taught and lectured in Egypt, Thailand and Japan and at eighteen different European universities, and been a Scholar in Residence at Symbiosis International University, Pune, and a Visiting Professor at American College, Madurai. He is a novelist, a playwright, and a classical numismatist. Among Dr. Jarman's "Indian" publications are a play, A Star Fell *(1998), about the events in Cawnpore (Kanpur) in 1857; a study of* sati, *or "widow-burning" (2002); and a biography of Azimullah Khan (2008).*

I

Diversity is about difference: it implies the existence of those who are not like us. While we may think that we know how to deal with our own kind, dealing with those who are different from us is a far more complex matter.

Their alterity (Otherness) is *threatening*. For most of human history, the lives of human beings have tended to be, as Thomas Hobbes (1651) famously put it, "solitary, poore, nasty, brutish, and short" (89). Most people were (and still are?) too weak and too insecure to be able to deal confidently with the unfamiliar or the unexpected. "Different" therefore tends to be seen as "dangerous".

But alterity can also be *convenient*. If we deny that others are like us, it becomes much easier to instrumentalise them, turning *people* into *things* and taking cruel advantage of them without letting human sympathy get in the way.

The most notorious historical example of this was probably the Atlantic Slave Trade of the 16th-19th centuries. Jean-Jacques Rousseau (1761) saw how the ruthless exploitation of African slaves for plantation labour in the Americas was only possible because they had been dehumanised, and he wrote that "on beholding one quarter of my fellow creatures *transformed into beasts for the service of the rest*, I could not forbear lamenting that I was a man" (II, 207, my italics).

Just occasionally, humanity *did* get in the way of instrumentalising the slaves, as happened to Philip Thicknesse, an 18th-century British visitor to the Caribbean:

> I once saved a beautiful girl from being soundly whipped! She paid me sometime afterwards in a manner I ought now to blush at, but when I offered to pay her for the kindness she had shown me, she absolutely refused and said, "No massa, my heart beat true for you." But yet surely they ought to be slaves, for do they not prefer a necklace of glass to one of solid gold? Have they not flatt noses and thick lips, and did they not fire upon me and wound me [...] only for going to hunt them a little in the Blue Mountains with fifty or sixty soldiers? (quoted in Ransford 1971, 119).

Turning human beings into things could also lead to awkward practical consequences. In the newly-founded United States of America, it was proposed that taxation should be levied on the basis of population. If the slaves were property, comparable to sheep, cattle or furniture, their masters wouldn't have to pay tax on them, but then neither would the slaves be counted in the census of the population (which determined how many political representatives from each State would be sent to Congress). The slave-owning Southern States therefore suggested that the slaves be counted as *people* for purposes of political representation, but as *property* for purposes of taxing their masters. Representatives of States where there were few slaves understandably said "No". In the notorious Three-Fifths Compromise of 1787 it was consequently agreed to count only 60% of the slave population.

Frank Tannenbaum (1946) has argued that slavery in Catholic Latin America was milder than it was in the Protestant north because of the centuries of human contact that the Spanish and Portuguese had previously had with Moors and Africans (through domestic, not plantation, slavery); also, because the North Americans were more radically different in skin colour to their slaves than the Hispanics were, with the white / black contrast easily seen as expressing godliness versus sinfulness.

Even today, whenever people "need" to be killed or their deaths can't be prevented, it is convenient to instrumentalise them rather than admit their humanity. During World War II, the Japanese Army in Manchuria subjected prisoners (both Chinese and Western) to grotesque and sadistic "medical" experiments. The prisoners who were tortured and murdered by Unit 731 were referred to as *maruta*, or "logs of wood"—they were not human beings (Daws 1994, 259). And in more recent wars, enemy or alien civilians accidentally injured or killed in military action have been described as "collateral damage". (Note that the term "collateral damage" is never applied to our own people, who are "innocent victims" of course.)

That which is other is to be feared, and it can also be exploited or taken for granted. The question of how to deal with the Other, wrote Carlos Fuentes in 1992, would be "the universal question of the coming century" (348). But how is that alterity defined?

II

The Franco-Bulgarian writer and philosopher Tzvetan Todorov has described (1982, 185) three levels or dimensions for determining Otherness:

a) We make a *value judgement* (the "axiological level"), *e.g.*, that the Other is inferior to us.

b) We make an *identification* (the "praxeological level"), assessing how much we share with the Other, *e.g.*, Do I impose my values and identity on the Other, or do I look for myself in the mirror of the Other?

c) We rely on our *knowledge*—or our ignorance—of the Other (the "epistemic level").

When European settlers first encountered Native Americans, they thus "explained" them in two different ways: as being intrinsically inferior to the Europeans (= a); or as being similar to Europeans, but childish and undeveloped (= b). Both these responses were grounded on ignorance (= c), as was the recurring idealisation or sentimentalisation of Native Americans as "Noble Savages". But "What [was] denied [was] the existence of a human substance truly other, something capable of being not merely an imperfect state of oneself" (42).

What is it that makes the Other *other*? There are a number of areas in which people have been sensitive to Otherness, using the perceived differences to distinguish between a safe "Us" and a strange or threatening or exotic or inferior "Them".

Strictly speaking, there is only one race of humans, *Homo sapiens*, the human species, but **race** has been an excuse for fear and hatred down the centuries, culminating in the ridiculous pseudo-scientific "master race" theories of modern times.

An important factor in the perception of "racial" Otherness has been **appearance**. In practice, this has usually meant skin colour, but sometimes also facial features or hair type. Westerners were formerly disturbed by the blackness of Africans (black being held to be the colour of the Devil). Yet the ancient Greeks and Romans were not particularly troubled by the appearance of Africans or Arabs, and seem not to have been colour-prejudiced. As Sir Alfred Zimmern pointed out, more than a century ago (1911), in a magisterial footnote:

> The Greeks thought negroes very interesting-looking people and were amused at their woolly hair, but they [showed] no trace of "colour-prejudice". [...] The sentiment of the "colour-bar" appears to be of comparatively recent origin [...] (323, footnote 1).

For their part, the Romans had (if anything) a mild prejudice against clumsy, pale-skinned Northern barbarians, but no prejudice against dark-skinned peoples (Snowden 1970, who provides substantial documentation of Greek and Roman attitudes to race).

The classical world thus lacked that "fundamental race distinction which became a marked characteristic of American Negro slavery of the 18th and 19th centuries" (Westermann 1955, 11). There was no mutually reinforcing semantic nexus of race, slavery and inferiority, since slaves in antiquity could be recruited from any social class and from any ethnic group. Nor was there any need to dehumanise them in order to exploit them (as the Christian world later found it necessary to do), because their enslavement stood in no contradiction to any widely accepted moral or religious precept of equality or human brotherhood.

Yet skin-colour obsession is not unique to the West. In much of Asia, darker skin colour is viewed as indicative of coolie status ("burnt dark by outdoor work in the sun") or of aboriginal origins. Many East and South East Asians also abhor extreme *paleness*, such as the whiteness of Western "foreign devils", who are the colour of ghosts, they believe (the Cantonese term for "Caucasian", "*gwailo*", literally means "ghost man"); and they dislike the comparative **hairiness** of Westerners. On travels in rural Thailand, I was pursued on several occasions by village children rudely calling out "Monkey, Monkey!", and even trying to pluck at the hairs on my forearms.

Then there is the matter of **smell**. Northern Europeans and North Americans sometimes complain about the "smelliness" of Africans in crowded places like trains, buses and aircraft, but to many Japanese it is also Westerners who smell disgusting ("*bata-kusai*", or "stinking-of-butter"), while their neighbours, the Koreans, who like their food much spicier than the Japanese do, are referred to disparagingly as "garlic stinkers".

The different **languages** that we speak make us seem different to each other. The ancient Greeks were disturbed by the inability of the "barbarians" (literally, the "ba-ba-speakers") to speak Greek properly, a failing taken as evidence of their inferiority. That included people who pretended to be Greeks but weren't really, like the people of Soloi in remote Cilicia, who spoke a comparatively corrupt form of the Greek language. From the term "*soloikismos*" comes the modern English word "solecism" (meaning, to break rules of good speech or behaviour).

The Macedonians, who spoke only a dialect of Greek, were similarly scorned. In his *Third Olynthiac*, the orator Demosthenes lambasted King Philip of Macedon: "Is not Philip our enemy? And in possession of our property? And a barbarian? Is any description too bad for him?" (51). Indeed,

> he is not only no Greek, but not even a barbarian from any place that can be named with honour! He is a pestilent knave from Macedon, from where it was never possible even to buy a decent slave (*Third Philippic*, 241, 243).

Differences in **social behaviour** can be the cause of contempt and detestation. To stay with the previous example, to the "civilised" Athenians, the Macedonians were disgusting in almost every respect, from their "lavish consumption of undiluted wine" (Doherty 2004, 8) to their custom of purifying their warriors "by marching [them] between the corpse of a dog, disembowelled and cut in half by a priest" (7).

To take a more modern example, a subject that today is almost taboo in public discourse but which surfaces constantly in private conversation in intercultural contexts is the culturally determined divide between those who clean their behinds with paper and those who do it with water and their left hand—with a striking lack of comprehension on both sides of the divide.

It is often hard to separate abhorrence of particular social behaviour from the **religious context** in which it takes place (or is supposed to take place). For instance, fictions about the vile customs and rituals of the Jews played a key role in anti-Semitism for hundreds of years, and in his *Gulliver's Travels* (1726), Jonathan Swift satirised the mutual intolerance of Protestants and Catholics as a conflict over which end a soft-boiled egg should be broken at:

> It is computed, that eleven thousand persons have, at several times, suffered death, rather than submit to break their eggs at the smaller end. Many hundred large volumes have been published upon this controversy: but the books of the Big-Endians have been long forbidden, and the whole party rendered incapable by law of holding employments (34-35).

Having the 'wrong' religious belief can indeed be enough to put others beyond hope. Priests and holy books have told us that the unbelievers are different, and that we should persecute them without mercy, and even exterminate them. Up to and including the present day, there has never been any shortage of fanatics to put such policies into practice.

The Turkish poet Ahmedi (*c.*1410) defined the *ghazi*, the Muslim warrior or "sword of God", as "the instrument of the religion of Allah, a servant of God who purifies the earth from the filth of polytheism" (quoted in Luttrell 1965, 139, "polytheism", because of the Christian belief in the Trinity). The killers of the so-called "Islamic State" are part of this tradition.

There were Christians, too, who were no less emphatic. In a war of extermination against French heretics, Catholic knights at the siege and sack of Béziers (1209) were confused by the physical and cultural similarity of their enemies; their leader, the warrior-priest Arnald-Amaury of Citeaux, supposedly advised them: "Kill them all! Afterwards, God will recognise His own!" (Sumption 1978, 93).

Unbelievers will burn in hell, according to the sacred texts of both Christianity and Islam.

> But the fearful, and unbelieving, and the abominable, and murderers, and whoremongers, and sorcerers, and idolators, And all liars, shall have their part in the lake which burneth with fire and brimstone: which is the second death (*Holy Bible, Revelation*, 21: 8, as with the following quotations, this is from the King James Version).

> Lo! Allah hath cursed the disbelievers, and hath prepared for them a flaming fire, / Wherein they will abide for ever (*Holy Koran,* 33:64 f., as with the following quotations, this is from the Pickthall translation).

> But as for those who disbelieve, garments of fire will be cut out for them; boiling fluid will be poured down on their heads (*Holy Koran*, 22:19).

> Lo! Those who disbelieve Our revelations, We shall expose them to the Fire. As often as their skins are consumed We shall exchange them for fresh skins that they may taste the torment. Lo! Allah is ever Mighty, Wise (*Holy Koran*, 4:56).

So why not just kill them *now*? The holy books seem to encourage this drastic way of thinking.

> And they entered into a covenant to seek the Lord God of their fathers with all their heart and soul; that whomsoever would not seek the Lord God of Israel should be put to death, whether small or great, whether man or woman *(Holy Bible, 2 Chronicles*, 12-13).

> But those mine enemies, which would not that I should reign over them, bring [them] hither, and slay them before me (*Holy Bible, Luke*, 19: 27).

> So make those who believe stand firm. I will throw fear into the hearts of those who disbelieve. Then smite the necks and smite of them each finger (*Holy Koran*, 8:12).

> [...] slay the idolaters wherever ye find them, and take them captive, and besiege them, and prepare for them each ambush (*Holy Koran*, 9:5).

In the context of India, **caste** has likewise been a major generator of hatred, intolerance and discrimination.

Interaction between the **generations** can also resemble communication cross-cultural barriers, involving as it may do an encounter between mutually incomprehensible values and attitudes. Twenty-four centuries ago, Plato in his *Republic* put the following words into the mouth of Socrates, enumerating forms of good behaviour, long forgotten, that the young people of Athens would do well to re-learn,

> [such as the] silence of the younger in the presence of their elders, which is becoming; and giving place to them and rising before them, and honouring their parents; the cut of the hair, the manner of dress and footgear, their whole bearing and deportment, and everything of that sort (223).

Men and women have been seen not only as being of different biological gender, but as belonging to different **gender cultures**. It is no secret that there are a lot of men who don't truly like or understand women—or who deeply fear them. There are also women who hate and despise men, though few have taken it to quite such bizarre lengths as the American radical feminist Valerie Solanas did, with her "Society for Cutting Up Men" (1967). Can men and women even communicate with each other? Communication between men and women (or the lack of it) has been studied by linguists like Deborah Tannen (*Gender and Discourse*, 1994), and described in popular bestsellers like John Gray's *Men Are from Mars, Women Are from Venus* (1992).

In many countries, people with a different **sexual orientation** to the mainstream are now no longer obliged to hide their preference, and Summerfield & Lee (2006) include "gay culture" in their study of American cultures, alongside the recognised cultural styles and behaviour patterns of the so-called "hyphenated Americans" (Italian-Americans, Irish-Americans, Japanese-Americans, and so on). Yet throughout the world, from the United States to East Africa to Iran, perceived sexual alterity is still a major cause of hatred and out-grouping ("homophobia"), often culminating in savage attacks on homosexuals.

When it comes to finding a loathsome Other to detest, despise or fear, there is no end to human ingenuity: the "class enemy"; the "Untouchable"; the fans of the hated rival football club; the "Prods" and "Taigs" in Northern Ireland; the Shi'a "dogs and donkeys" and the Sunni, "worse than dogs"; the Australian "Abos"; the Mexican-American "wetbacks"; the Romani "Gyppos" (and the non-Romani "Gadjos"); the "Eternal Jew". The Other offers frightened or immature human beings a convenient surface onto which to project their terrors and repressed longings. But even after those demons have been exorcised, even after we have come to terms with childhood fears and emotions, we cannot do without alterity in our lives. There is still an underlying, vital function for the Other to fulfil.

If it is constructed positively, our relationship with the Other in its various forms will be the most important one we shall ever have, because it enables us to establish the parameters of our identity. Anida Yoeu Ali, a Cambodian-American performance artist of mixed Malaysian Muslim, Thai, Khmer and Cham (!) origin, stated it very clearly in a recent BBC interview: "Your difference is what makes you who you are!" This is the *only* means by which we can grow, since it is through the Other that we achieve the Self.

Drawing on the ideas of the philosopher Martin Buber, the psychologist Erik Erikson, and the biologist-cyberneticians Humberto Maturana and Francisco Varela, the German theologian and educationalist Peter Graf (2011) has written:

> No person is able to find his identity on his own: he will only achieve this in interaction with and in relation to others. The self-image is only convincing when discovered as a reflection in the mirror of the Other. Nobody fixes his identity before turning his attention to the Other. On the contrary, he only realises what he might be through the reaction of others (21).

It's time for us to have the courage to enter into a dialogue with the Other, and to celebrate diversity and learn from it, not persecute it. A nation that can draw upon the intellectual resources of multiple groups, a country whose dominant culture and minorities have learned to live together peacefully, is truly blessed. It will be in a position to enjoy all the benefits of dialogue-fuelled creativity, of forward-looking synergistic cooperation—what the economic journalist Pascal Zachary (2003) has called the "diversity advantage".

Let us therefore turn our attention to India, the most spectacular example of diversity to be found anywhere in the world.

III

No large country can compete with India in the range and number of its ethnic and cultural groups, its religions, castes, languages, climates and landscapes. It is almost too much for a single imagination to comprehend, and it defies generalisation, except on the *kitsch* level of curries, maharajahs, gurus, tigers and turbans.

Visitors to India, including its conquerors, have often been overwhelmed. The negative comments by the Mughal invader Babur in the *Baburnama* (beginning "Hindustan is a country of few charms", 518) have been quoted many times, which is unfair, because this section on "The Defects of Hindustan" is immediately balanced by a following section on "The Advantages of Hindustan", and both are part of a long and often enthusiastic description of Babur's new kingdom that also contains the statement "It is a wonderful country" (484).

The most famous description of the diversity of India is probably Rudyard Kipling's affectionate account in *Kim* (1901) of life on the Grand Trunk Road. Kim and the lama have encountered an old soldier, who tells them:

> "All castes and kinds of men move here. Look! Brahmins and chumars [leather workers—*Ed.*], bankers and tinkers, barbers and bunnias [shopkeepers—*Ed.*], pilgrims and potters—all the world going and coming. It is to me as a river from which I am withdrawn like a log after a flood."
>
> And truly the Grand Trunk Road is a wonderful spectacle. It runs straight, bearing without crowding India's traffic for fifteen hundred miles—such a river of life as nowhere else exists in the world (105).

The lama's gaze is turned inward to spiritual matters, seeking the fabled River of the Arrow, and not the "river of life". But Kim is already observant, even though he has not yet been schooled in observation by the spymaster Lurgan Sahib as part of his preparation for the "Great Game".

> [...] Kim's bright eyes were open wide. This broad, smiling river of life, he considered, was a vast improvement on the cramped and crowded Lahore streets. There were new people and new sights at every stride—castes he knew and castes that were altogether out of his experience.
>
> They met a troop of long-haired, strong-scented Sansis [a nomadic tribe—*Ed.*] with baskets of lizards and other unclean food on their backs, their lean dogs sniffing at their heels. These people kept their own side of the road, moving at a quick, furtive jog-trot, and all other castes gave them ample room; for the Sansi is deep pollution. Behind them, walking wide and stiffly across the strong shadows, the memory of his leg-irons still on him, strode one newly released from the jail; his full stomach and shiny skin to prove that the Government fed its prisoners better than most honest men could feed themselves. Kim knew that walk well, and made broad jest of it as they passed. Then an Akali, a wild-eyed, wild-haired Sikh devotee in the blue-checked clothes of his faith, with polished-steel quoits glistening on the cone of his tall blue turban, stalked past, returning from a visit to one of the independent Sikh States, where he had been singing the ancient glories of the Khalsa to College-trained princelings in top-boots and white-cord breeches. Kim was careful not to irritate that man; for the Akali's temper is short and his arm quick. Here and there they met or were overtaken by the gaily dressed crowds of whole villages turning out to some local fair; the women, with their babes on their hips, walking behind the men, the older boys prancing on sticks of sugar-cane, dragging rude brass models of locomotives such as they sell for a halfpenny, or flashing the sun into the eyes of their betters from cheap toy mirrors. One could see at a glance what each had bought; and if there were any doubt, it needed only to watch the wives comparing, brown arm against brown arm, the newly purchased dull glass bracelets that come from the North-West. These merry-makers stepped slowly, calling one to the other and stopping to haggle with sweetmeat-sellers, or to make a prayer before one of the

> wayside shrines—sometimes Hindu, sometimes Mussalman—which the low-caste of both creeds share with beautiful impartiality. A solid line of blue, rising and falling like the back of a caterpillar in haste, would swing up through the quivering dust and trot past to a chorus of quick cackling. That was a gang of *changars* [labourers—*Ed.]*—the women who have taken all the embankments of all the Northern railways under their charge—a flat-footed, big-bosomed, strong-limbed, blue-petticoated clan of earth-carriers, hurrying north on news of a job, and wasting no time by the road. They belong to the caste whose men do not count, and they walked with squared elbows, swinging hips, and heads on high, as suits women who carry heavy weights. A little later, a marriage procession would strike into the Grand Trunk with music and shoutings, and a smell of marigold and jasmine stronger even than the reek of the dust. [...]
>
> The lama never raised his eyes. He did not note the moneylender on his goose-rumped pony, hastening along to collect the cruel interest; or the long-shouting, deep-voiced little mob—still in military formation—of native soldiers on leave, rejoicing to be rid of their breeches and puttees, and saying the most outrageous things to the most respectable women in sight. Even the seller of Ganges-water he did not see, and Kim expected that he would at least buy a bottle of that precious stuff. He looked steadily at the ground, and strode as steadily hour after hour, his soul busied elsewhere. But Kim was in the seventh heaven of joy. The Grand Trunk at this point was built on an embankment to guard against winter floods from the foothills, so that one walked, as it were, a little above the country, along a stately corridor, seeing all India spread out to left and right (109-11).

The gadfly Indian critic Nirad C. Chaudhuri (1957) notoriously put on record that he considered *Kim* to be "the finest novel in the English language with an Indian theme" (47), compounding his gleeful provocation of Indian literary sensibilities a few years later (1965) when he expressed the opinion that Kipling was the only English writer who would have "a permanent place in English literature with books on Indian themes" and that *Kim* would be read "by anyone who [wanted] to know not only *British* India but also *timeless* India" (8, the emphases are in the original).

Despite Kim's (and his creator's) obvious delight in the colour, life and diversity of India, there is no doubt that all of it is subservient to the Raj, just as Kim—even though he grew up in the bazaars and back-streets of Lahore—diligently serves the interests of the British in India (which are in any case also the best interests of the native population, paternalistic imperialists might add).

This is made even clearer in the story "Her Majesty's Servants" (in *The Jungle Book*, 1894), in which the animals who are the anthropomorphic protagonists of the tale, battery-mules, baggage-camels, troop-horses, gun-bullocks and gun-elephants, despite all their differences, still play their parts loyally in a great parade that is put on to dazzle (and intimidate) the visiting Amir of Afghanistan. An Indian "native officer" explains to a "Central Asian chief":

> "They obey, as the men do. Mule, horse, elephant, or bullock, he obeys his driver, and the driver his sergeant, and the sergeant his lieutenant, and the lieutenant his captain, and the captain his major, and the major his colonel, and the colonel his brigadier commanding three regiments, and the brigadier the general, who obeys the Viceroy, who is the servant of the Empress. Thus it is done."
>
> "Would it were so in Afghanistan!" said the chief; "for there we obey only our own wills."
>
> "And for that reason," said the native officer, twirling his moustache, "your Amir whom you do not obey must come here and take orders from our Viceroy" (179).

Does it really take an outsider to appreciate and enjoy the diversity of India? (Kipling, who was born in Bombay and who throughout his life remained fascinated by arcana and "insider knowledge", would not necessarily have seen himself as an outsider.) Are most Indians themselves hampered in doing so by their commitment to a particular religious, regional or caste identity?

Describing India's diversity is difficult enough—how then is such rich complexity to be *ruled*? Babur's grandson Akbar understood the danger of the Hindu / Muslim divide, and in 1579 he sensibly abolished the hated *jiziya* tax on non-Muslims. He went out of his way to accommodate and reassure his Hindu subjects:

> As his reign progressed, Akbar continued to make deliberate concessions to Hindu customs—introducing their festivals at court and having newly washed and painted cows brought into his presence after Diwali, letting his hair grow long in a Hindu fashion and adopting a Rajput style of turban, even on occasions wearing the *tilak*, the Hindu sectarial or ornamental mark made on the forehead—until the more orthodox Muslims became convinced that the emperor had abandoned their faith (Gascoigne 1971, 82).

His successor Jahangir continued many of his father's tolerant policies, so much so that the English Ambassador to the Mughal court, Sir Thomas Roe, who was in India from 1615 to 1619, noted (not quite accurately) that "all sorts of religions are wellcome and free, for the king is of none" (quoted in Mukhia 2004, 20).

Independent India's new rulers made the wise decision not to take the Pakistani route: they would *not* cast the fledgling country into a narrow religious mould. The Pakistan government is now [2015] even compounding their original disastrous decision by trying to force the country in a dubious linguistic direction as well, replacing English wherever possible with Urdu (which is itself a minority language in Pakistan, albeit one of high status), a further move backwards into chauvinism and obscurantism.

Ramachandra Guha has noted Nehru's "refusal to reduce India or 'Indianness' to a dominant religious or linguistic ethos" (2012), and he describes a significant exchange of letters between Nehru and Vallabhbhai Patel, immediately after Independence, on the question of retribution for the atrocities committed against Hindu refugees fleeing Pakistan.

> Their voice was loud, and for many, compelling. But Nehru told his home minister and close co-worker that it must be quelled: for, India, if it was anything at all, was emphatically *not* Pakistan. Over there, they might ill-treat or persecute their minorities; over here, we would protect and respect ours. There was, wrote Nehru to Patel, "a constant cry for retaliation and vicarious punishment of the Muslims of India, because the Pakistanis punish Hindus. That argument does not appeal to me in the slightest". For India was not a mirror image of Pakistan, a Hindu state to its Islamic state. "Our secular ideals," insisted Nehru to Patel, "impose a responsibility to our Muslim citizens in India" (139-40).

The secular toleration of diversity and alterity was not merely an imperative of decency or an idealistic vision; it was also a practical necessity, in order to keep an at the time fairly ramshackle State that was really a subcontinent from simply tearing itself apart. Yet it was perhaps also a premonition of potential greatness, for if such manifold traditions and philosophies, ways of thinking, behaving and interacting with the world, such diverse beliefs, hopes and dreams could somehow be harnessed together in the name of a single unifying cause—India perceived as *Bharat*, so to speak, rather than India as *Hindustan*—it might one day, lead to exciting synergies rather than conflicts.

That vision is now being challenged, not only by Jihadi terrorists but also by the ideologues of Hindutva. In an editorial article in *The Economist* that tried, in the light of the destruction of the Babri Masjid in Ayodha in December 1992, to explain what it called the "The Hindu Upsurge", its authors noted that the time was now gone when "militant Hinduism [...] evoked yawns and amused smiles" (22), but warned against widespread misconceptions about the nature of the phenomenon.

> One [of these misconceptions, they wrote] is that the problem in India is a Hindu-Muslim one. In fact, it is an argument between secular and communal Hindus over the treatment of Muslims. [...] The main critics of Hindu militancy, measured in numbers, are secular Hindus, not Muslims (24).

Another misconception was that the militants were committed to a fundamentalist agenda, to taking India back into the Middle Ages. But in historical terms, a genuinely fundamentally Hindu India might prove to be a fairly tolerant place, and, anyway,

> that is not the BJP's aim. It wants to transform Hinduism from an amorphous collection of quarrelsome groups into an organised society fit for the 21st century—a unified Hinduism such as has never existed (*ibid.*).

Far from seeking to split India, the authors claimed, the BJP believed that Hindu nationalism was the glue to hold it together. Its supporters rejected comparisons with the Nazi movement in Germany at the end of Weimar, but the Hindu militant slogan of "one nation, one culture, one religion, one language" is nevertheless chillingly reminiscent of the Nazi mantra *Ein Volk, ein Reich, ein Führer* (one people, one realm, one leader).

One nation? Certainly, India is a country bursting at the seams with promise.

One culture? No one who has travelled extensively in India believes that it is a monoculture, and trying to impose that condition on the nation would only impoverish it.

One religion? Obviously not. And why should there be? The Pakistani model is hardly encouraging. India as a Hindu twin (Nehru's "mirror image") to its northern Muslim neighbour, with Hinduism as the State religion? (Though which *form* of Hinduism?) Non-Hindus excluded from high positions in the state and the legal system? The death penalty for blasphemy?

And one language? India has a linguistic embarrassment of riches, and every single one of the languages, however small the number of its native speakers, is a cultural treasure-house. The linguistic situation in India is complex and demanding, to be sure, but attempts to impose Hindi on the Dravidian South, for example, are an arrogant affront and a recipe for disaster. (Incidentally, how would Hindi-speakers enjoy having Tamil or Telugu imposed on *them*?)

In a speech in New Delhi on January 28th, 2015, Prime Minister Narendra Modi declared:

> Our country is full of diversities, and unity in diversity is the beauty and strength of our nation. And this is what keeps inspiring us ("Unity in diversity is strength of our nation"—PM Modi, online)

and he made a similar statement in an interview with *Time* magazine in May:

> The diversity of India, of our civilisation, is actually a thing of beauty, which is something we are extremely proud of. [...] So far as the government is concerned, there is only one holy book, which is the Constitution of India ("We Are Natural Allies", online).

India's complex diversity is potentially a world-beating resource. Nick Clayton (2015) quotes the view of venture capitalist Venktesh Shukla that diversity is ingrained in a country where even in small villages there may be multiple languages spoken, and several religions and types of local cuisine. Indeed: "If you've grown up in India, you instinctively know people are different, not superior, just different." And Sunil Khilnani has based a BBC 'Radio 4 series' (2015), and now a book, *Incarnations* (2016), on the premise that India's diversity is a treasure, and its complex history, riddled with contradictions, not a threat but something that is enabling (Biswas 2016).

Yet while the message of synergistic diversity is one that educated, Aspirational India no doubt wants to hear, and the international community, too, will it go down so well with Modi's core voters on the Hindu Right? Can Modi's government be trusted? The events that have unfolded since the election are far from reassuring.

India is now at a crossroads.

After the Election—What Next?

Rakesh Sharma

*The overwhelming election victory of the BJP in 2014 raised all kinds of questions about which direction India would now take, and which political, social and cultural models it would follow. In September 2014, filmmaker Rakesh Sharma (*Final Solution*, 2004, winner of the Wolfgang Staudte Prize at the Berlin International Film Festival) was interviewed by Anupama Katakam.*

Question: The BJP won the 2014 polls comprehensively. What worked for them?

First and foremost, the Congress deserves much credit for the BJP's electoral success. Corruption, inept governance, terrible perception management and atrocious media strategy during the UPA 2 regime only sharpened the natural anti-incumbency any party would face after 10 years in power.

Secondly, the 2014 polls saw 100 million first-time voters. Another 120 million were second-time voters, *i.e.*, approximately 220 million of the 815 million eligible voters were young Indians. They form a majority within what I'd call the Aspirational India Block, which also has others—urban populations, especially middle-class professionals and businessmen in the 25-45 demographic. Post-poll analysis seems to suggest that the BJP won this block overwhelmingly.

Thirdly, we saw a remarkable campaign by Team Modi, not just through their public rallies and TV / online ads, but also through their media management skills. They hammered in a core message: The Congress has messed up, they're corrupt and indecisive, and they're unable to provide either a vision or a strong leader. Modi is decisive, above corruption, a strong man to helm the nation during a crisis. Add to it their political savvy, especially in election management, and some smart politics in the run-up to the polls (*e.g.*, alliances like Apna Dal in Uttar Pradesh, the splitting of Satnami votes in Chhattisgarh, *etc.*). No wonder they won so comprehensively!

Question: How much did the right-wing / communal agenda play a part and how much would you say was just anti-incumbency?

I think it had become largely untenable for anyone to justify UPA 2 or support them or ask for votes in their name.

The Congress also managed to successfully decimate its sole USP of being the "natural party for governance". Whether it was the Janata Party regime, the coalitions of the mid-Nineties or even the Vajpayee government that lost the 2004 polls, the perception among the electorate was: Congress knows how to govern, and it has fifty years of experience, whereas the others flounder and pander to coalition compulsions. This perception took a severe beating in the years leading up to the 2014 polls, as they floundered terribly and succumbed to what the party called "coalition dharma".

It is no secret that the anti-corruption movement saw the active participation of the right wing's cadres—this helped shape the "mood of the nation". The Nirbhaya case-related protests and the UPA's bungling responses only sharpened this mood. Team Modi capitalised on it brilliantly. It ended up reaping even the AAP's potential electoral harvest.

Mr. Modi's team created the perception of a void in national politics. His campaign showcased the UPA's terrible failings while hammering in a single message—*Main Hoon Naa,* I'll come and fix everything!

Of course, the core ideology of his party too came into electoral play, but mostly in pockets like Uttar Pradesh, where a sharp polarisation was needed to triumph over identity politics practised by caste-based formulations like Mayawati's BSP or Mulayam's SP.

Question: What about their ground-level electoral management?

It was nothing short of brilliant, an object lesson for other parties. The Modi-Shah combine showcased their masterly skill, honed over three state elections in Gujarat.

I'll cite just one example from battleground Uttar Pradesh, where the NDA won 73 out of 80 seats, an unprecedented electoral success.

Each sheet in the electoral rolls has 30 names—a two-sided sheet *(Panna)* has 60 voters. They appointed one *Panna Prahbari* (loosely translated as Page-in-charge) per sheet, responsible for a block of 60 votes. In any electoral booth with a total of 1000-1200 votes, they had 15-20 *Panna Prabharis*! That's a remarkable degree of detailing and management! And they have the cadres for it.

No party has such numbers of ideologically committed cadres, apart from the Left, which too, is battling a crisis in West Bengal, while holding on to its space in Kerala.

Question: Uttar Pradesh has traditionally been split up between the SP, BSP, Congress and the BJP. Were there other factors in play too?

Like UPA 2, the Akhilesh government too was presented as being corrupt, inefficient and inept. This played a key part in the BJP's landslide win. To understand more, we need to delve into the state's electoral history.

During 1989-91, I'd done a film for Channel 4 (UK), looking at the collapse of centrist politics and the emergence of the right wing, especially in Uttar Pradesh, where it won the state elections. After that Kalyan Singh government, the BJP went into a steady decline, eclipsed by the dominance of caste politics that grabbed the space vacated by the centrist polity, splitting its vote banks among them.

Interestingly, both these strands of identity-politics have been in a tug of war. Caste proved to be the graveyard of Hindutva politics as it punctured the basic tenet itself—see yourself as a Hindu first, then unite and vote as Hindus. The SP and BSP (with its *Tilak, Tarazu aur Talwar, inko maaro jootey chaar*, Hit the Brahmins, Thakurs and Banias with shoes! *i.e.*, Down with upper castes!) posited their caste identity against the BJP construct of a pan-Hindu identity. This time the BJP needed to reverse the trend here, so that the caste identity could be subsumed by Hindutva. It needed communal polarisation to get Dalit, OBC and EBC votes—the 2013 Muzaffarnagar riots and the ongoing *Love Jihad* campaign [Muslim men targeting non-Muslim women "romantically" to win them to Islam—*Ed.*] underscore this strategy.

Question: It appears that these divisive politics are leading to a growing sense of fear among minorities. As someone who has filmed the outcome of a right-wing agenda, could you comment on this?

Yes, it appears that minorities are now experiencing the sort of fear their Gujarati brethern experienced ten–fifteen years ago. It'll settle into a similar pattern—some will make peace with the devil, vote for it, rush to proclaim their loyalty especially at showcased public events; some others will support anybody-but-the-BJP, many would become apathetic and some will be drawn into their own campaigns of hate, intolerance and bigotry or even violence.

But we need to see the right-wing agenda from a wider perspective. The BJP's relentless campaign since the late 1980s has helped it raise its tally from two MPs to 282 MPs! Its agenda now is to consolidate itself both in lost territories like Uttar Pradesh and new territories like Eastern India.

So we are now witnessing a differential set of strategies for different regions or different interest groups.

UP saw a consolidation against the Muslim voters, especially among Jats and Dalits of the Muzaffarnagar belt, with the BJP weaning them away from Ajit Singh or Mayawati. The *Love Jihad* strategy is taking it state-wide, into every district, with the known rabble-rouser Yogi Adityanath as the chosen messenger.

For the young voter of the Aspirational India Block, it is Modi, the *Vikaspurush*, or "man of development", who'll fix the economy, create jobs and business opportunities and provide corruption-free good governance. So we heard *ad nauseum* about the so-called Gujarat model, even when analysts and commentators pointed out that Gujarat lagged behind on several social indices or that other states were ahead on economy-related parameters like FDI, *etc.*

Now we're witnessing a longer term image makeover. As opposed to the "remote-controlled" Manmohan Singh, Modi is the decisive leader. His omnipotence is now taking on all sorts of hues—the leader the world bows to, the leader who knows how to decisively answer arch-enemy Pakistan, the leader who cracks down on impropriety (*e.g.*, monitoring his own ministers), the avuncular leader who shares his memories directly with school children, plays the flute, beats drums—in essence, a jolly-natured pan-Indian patriarch with an iron grip.

Question: You speak about different strategies for different regions. Could you elaborate?

BJP doesn't need a sharp polarisation in Madhya Pradesh, for instance. So, the *Love Jihad* campaign stops at the Uttar Pradesh-Madhya Pradesh border. It isn't as if the state doesn't have inter-faith romances or marriages!

Gujarat saw a similar sharp campaign in the earlier phases—Babu Bajrangi rendered "social service" by kidnapping girls gone "astray", reuniting them with their Hindu families. The (late) Pavagadh *Pracharak* (full-time RSS activist) Prahlad Shastri used to rattle off *taluka*-wise (administrative section-wise) lists of cases (Hindu girls in Muslim homes) in his incendiary speeches. Post-2002, such campaigns were no longer necessary in the state.

The next serious battleground is Eastern India. In Bengal, Assam and parts of North East India, it wouldn't be surprising to find sharper and strident ground-level campaigns invoking the "outsider" versus "son of the soil"—the Bangladeshi Muslim immigrant versus the local. Such invocations have resulted in handsome dividends for the Right globally, where the "Other", *i.e.*, the enemy, is either the immigrant (Turk, Algerian or Moroccan) or the jihadist (Al-Qaeda, Taliban, ISIS or the local "Paki") or a combination thereof. The Sangh Parivar, over the years, has sporadically invoked the Bangladeshi bogey countrywide, but this is likely to intensify in Eastern India. West Bengal is likely to see a polarisation into BJP versus Mamata, with the Congress waning even in its own pocket boroughs, and the Left likely to become more and more inconsequential or, worse, forced to ally with a "secular" front.

Bihar too is a likely candidate for politics of polarisation, especially after the rather savvy and unexpected Nitish-Lalu alliance, which has turned the electoral math upside down.

Seemandhra is likely to remain insulated for now, as the BJP's ally Naidu is in power, but Telangana is ripe for staging such politics, once the euphoria over its statehood dies down. As an aside, this region amply illustrates the Congress' ineptitude—any party that created a new state, giving in to a decades-old demand, should've reaped major electoral benefits! Instead, in Telangana, even their ally the TRS went back on its electoral alliance promise, perhaps influenced by the sharp anti-Congress mood nationwide.

Kerala has always had RSS [the Hindu nationalist *Rashtriya Swayamsevak Sangh—Ed.*] pockets within this Left bastion, with pitched battles and political assassinations marking the terrain. As Congress becomes more and more irrelevant nationally, the BJP is likely to gain not just from the defectors, but also from a consolidation among non-Left electorates.

Tamil Nadu is likely to be the toughest to penetrate, especially as its major political streams emerged from a strong anti-brahminical ethos, represented by the DMK and later, the AIADMK. It is unlikely that the RSS brand of puritanical, brahminical Hindutva would flourish here. Rather than a strident advocacy of Hindutva, we may see a focused attempt to expand by seizing the opposition space that the DMK is likely to cede post-Karunanidhi, now that the prospect of a Stalin-Alagiri reconciliation is rather unlikely.

In Central India—Madhya Pradesh, Rajasthan, Chhattisgarh—the BJP is firmly entrenched. These states are unlikely to see strident politics. Here, the BJP will quietly focus on tightening its stranglehold, as it did in Gujarat.

Question: Gujarat is said to be the laboratory of the Hindu Nation. Why did Hindutva work so effectively in Gujarat? How did the political consolidation take place? Since you have covered the region extensively for over a decade, how do you see it?

First—the historical perspective. Gujarat has had a history of communal violence dating back to the late Sixties, with a cycle of riots marking each subsequent decade. Each such wave sharpened an anti-minority sentiment among the caste Hindus while at the same time creating a sense of fear and distrust among the minorities.

The right wing's mobilisations in the Eighties and early Nineties, for *Ramshilapujan* [the dedication of bricks for the rebuilding of the temple of Rama on the ruins of the mosque of Babur in Ayodhya—*Ed.*] and the *Karseva* [voluntary religious service—*Ed.*], found great success in Gujarat, especially among the middle class and the BJP's traditional support base of traders and upper castes. Later *karseva-in-Ayodhya* campaigns saw focused mobilisation among the recently proselytised tribals, brought back into the "Hindu" fold through that immense network of *Vanvasi Kalyan Kendras* [an organisation dedicated to the empowerment of tribal populations—*Ed.*]) and *Shishu Mandirs* [a network of schools with a traditionalist and Hindu nationalistic focus—*Ed.*]. In 2002, in Panchmahals, I found many of the mob leaders and riot-accused to be the earliest tribal cadres enlisted for the initial *karseva* campaigns of the early and mid-Nineties.

The collapse of the mills, especially in the "Manchester of Gujarat", Gomtipur in Ahmedabad, pushed thousands of workers into the abyss of unemployment, loss of hope, alcoholism and penury. Many died awaiting their legitimate dues and provident funds. Many Dalit-OBC workers, angry with the Congress, the party ruling the Centre and the State, turned away from it. A simultaneous collapse of Trade Unions saw the Left losing even the toehold it had. This was a fertile ground for right-wing recruitment and expansion. It is not surprising to note that a majority of the S-6 *karsevaks* in 2002 were from the working class, most of the casualties were OBCs.

Earlier, the Chimanbhai Patel government, seen in public perception as the most corrupt government ever, with its patronage of a notorious underworld don, Latif, paved the way in 1995 for the BJP's electoral forays. Madhavsinh Solanki's KHAM (Kshatriya, Harijan, Adivasi and Muslim) formula had alienated the Patels, a dominant caste grouping, with land ownership and a wide range of business interests—they turned into the BJP's early core supporters.

Once the BJP came into power, it consolidated its stranglehold, slowly but surely, decimating the Congress, and turning Gujarat into a virtual single-party state. Much of Congress politics right from the Gandhi-Patel era grew out of a strong network of co-operatives, many of them set up by erstwhile Gandhians. In the last decade and a half, the BJP has steadily taken over this space, assimilating dairy and farmer co-operatives, and taking over co-op banks.

The state has many quasi-religious networks. The BJP made strong inroads into sects like Pandurang Shastri Athavale's *Swadhyay* movement, with its base among the *Kolis* (a coastal community) and some tribal communities. People like Asaram Bapu regularly rubbed shoulders with the top BJP leadership (much of the YouTube footage has now vanished, including one where Asaram affectionately patted Modi's cheeks with the words: "I see Lord Krishna in him!"). Even the Swaminarayan sect's members began to support the BJP. In 2002, despite repeated meetings with his savvy staff, I was unable to get the Pramukh Swami to simply condemn the violence on camera!

If Gujarat is termed the "laboratory", we need to understand not just how it worked, but also the tremendous strategic effort that made it so successful.

Today, the Congress stands decimated, consigned to electoral insignificance, steadily losing cadres and ground in each election. But then, some of the credit must go to its own leaders, particularly those in the inner circle, who presided over its demise in Gujarat.

Question: Gujarat, however, is seen as a BJP success story, a sort of model to follow. What are some of the things you see in common with other BJP-ruled states?

Well—the usual first. Many from within the cadres or the sympathiser support base will get absorbed in the state machinery, be it recruitments into the police constabulary, homeguards or the state civil services. You might find a special emphasis on such absorption in primary and secondary school teacher and *shiksha-sahayak* (school assistant) recruitments.

There is likely to be greater patronage of Sangh Parivar organisations—many centres run by them turn into natural beneficiaries of government largesse: financial grants, cheap land, roads, *etc.*

But the tectonic shift happens away from these discernible actions—at ground level. Our system still works on the patronage-model, an overhang of our feudal past. The patronage can either be bought (bribes) or wangled through community and local networks. Whether it is to get a BPL card, Aadhar ID, a seed subsidy, a low-interest crop loan, a village check dam or pucca road—people need to get their work done through the local sarpanch or corporator or MLA. It is easier done through the ruling party reps. Once you're thus obligated, do you support or vote for any other party?

The present-day Congress has been out of power in Gujarat for four terms. As a party, it has been an opportune alliance of interests, rather than an ideologically-driven cadre-based party. The opportunists shift their allegiances once they themselves are bereft of such patronage and are, in turn, unable to provide patronage to their own support bases. They may wait for a term or two, but then the shift becomes expedient. In Gujarat, one of my oft-heard observations has been—he can't even get things done for himself, what will he do for us, when referring to the local Congressman.

Wherever the BJP has been in power for more than two consecutive terms, the Congress has been decimated—MP and Gujarat being the prime examples. As the Congress loses more state elections and is seen as being weak, unlikely to return to power, such a silent tectonic shift will happen, with the Congress reduced to a statistically significant but electorally irrelevant voteshare.

Question: People have been able to look past Modi and Shah being charged for not just communal violence but heinous crimes such as encounters. How did they shake off that label?

I think the more relevant point is what makes Indians look past this.

As a society, perhaps our defining trait is apathy. It is evident at various levels—"clean" home interiors with garbage merrily dumped on the street, or the belief of being above the everyday law (jumping queues, breaking traffic signals and suchlike), or in the erstwhile grudging and now blatant admiration of those who "bend" the system like the Ambanis. Its most common manifestation is to forget and move on. We want to bury unpleasant memories and experiences, be it molestation by an uncle within the extended family, or an accident victim we failed to help or the horrors of violence we witnessed. We have hardly dealt with the horrors of the 1947 Partition, unlike say, Germany, where the anti-Nazi discourse has been in the public realm—in literature, art, cinema, academia and even school textbooks. Perhaps that's why we're condemned to repeat our horrifying history, to paraphrase Santayana.

In addition to apathy, last couple of decades have seen the rise of latent communalism. These may be people who do not support a hardcore agenda, but are happy to have a no-Muslim-tenant society or a fully vegetarian complex, or they agitate for a meat-free McDonald's. Our urban spaces, including that great metropolis Bombay, are no melting pots, but are transforming into clusters of community-based ghettos or class-driven gated communities.

It is a very potent mix—apathy, latent communalism and blatant fundamentalism, especially if the fires are stoked to keep the cauldron boiling over.

Question: When you shot Final Solution, did you ever think the result of right-wing politics could lead to such carnage and destruction? That Modi's and the BJP's strategy had worked?

I saw the 2002 carnage as a turning point in our political history, the second phase of assertion of aggressive Hindutva, the first being the 1992 Babri Masjid demolition. I didn't, however, see Modi as a potential PM, despite the evident nature of his political ambitions.

When Modi swept the polls in 2007, and the image makeover began to take place (Vibrant Gujarat summits, the Tata Nano project, *etc.*), it began to seem possible; after filming the 2012 Gujarat elections, where I witnessed not just Modi's electoral pull, but the party's vice-like grip on election management and the Congress' flummoxed inability to be a challenger, it seemed inevitable. UPA 2 made such a mess in the last couple of years of its term that Modi seemed unstoppable. Even then, 282 seats and a majority for the BJP itself were a surprise—for which Modi's election machinery and managers need to be credited.

Question: As a keen observer of politics, how do you see the landscape ahead?

We are headed for very interesting times.

If the Congress doesn't re-invent itself and waits either for a 2004-like verdict that took the party by surprise or for the BJP to score enough own-goals to make people yearn for the Gandhis, then the party is headed towards terminal decline.

The opposition space ceded by it is up for grabs—the AAP could have been a serious contender, were they not prone to kneejerk campaigns, whimsical politics and an astounding lack of vision to turn their volunteer base into a democratic party with robust mechanisms in place.

If our earlier polity was marked by an aversion to the Congress, it is quite possible to witness a consolidation among electoral parties along the lines of anyone-but-BJP, especially if their own existence is threatened, with their support base being poached by the BJP.

The BJP itself is already on the cusp of an interesting dilemma. It swept the young Aspirational India electorate. Add another 120-140 million first time voters in 2019 to the 200-odd million now—and it is a serious block of 350 million voters (roughly 40% of the electorate). A Shining India Part 2 has been promised to them. How does the BJP reconcile this block with the anachronistic Sangh Parivar vision of Akhand Bharat, Hindutva and Swadeshi?

Or will the BJP break out of the RSS mould and morph into a centre-right party with pan-India appeal? Will it pay more than lip service and actually construct the Ayodhya Temple? Ban beef and alienate not just the minorities but a large Dalit population? Peddle *stree-dharma* (woman's duty) to promote the ancient *Bhartiya Nari* (Indian woman) ideal and alienate the modern Indian woman? How will they reconcile Swadeshi with their love for MNCs, MOUs signed in shiny / vibrant investment summits, GM crop trials, more FDI, even in hitherto protected sectors like Defence, *etc.*

How will the BJP tackle its own internal genetic contradictions? What will be the tensions, pulls and pressures? This dialectic interests me immensely as a student of history and politics.

Making the City Hers

Githa Hariharan

Githa Hariharan is a distinguished writer and commentator. Her first novel, The Thousand Faces of Night *(1993), was awarded the Commonwealth Writers' Prize, and her writing has been translated into many different languages. In 1995, she challenged the Hindu Minority and Guardianship Act as being discriminatory against women. The landmark case, Githa Hariharan and Another vs. Reserve Bank of India and Another, led to a Supreme Court judgement in 1999 on guardianship. For more on her work, see the website www.githahariharan.com.*

I must have been ten years old, on my way to school in a public BEST bus in what was then Bombay. As always, the bus was crowded with men and women on their way to work, but I had managed to get a seat. Suddenly, the woman in the seat across the aisle pulled a slipper off her foot, waved it threateningly, and brought it down on the man next to her. I did not know enough Marathi to understand what she was shouting at him. But soon, others in the bus joined the woman in roughing up the man. He was trying hard to shrink in his window seat and make himself as small as possible. Then the bus came to a halt and its citizens threw out the man. The bus that went on filled with an unspoken friendship; everyone seemed to be on the side of the woman. She still looked angry, but she was quiet now. She sat straight-shouldered, as if she knew exactly what the people in the bus, and the city at large, owed her.

It must have taken all of ten minutes, my first spectacle of what I would learn, many years later, to call "sexual harassment". The shouting and the man being beaten must have been frightening for a child, but at this distance, what I recall is my getting off the bus at school, feeling safe. What made me feel safe, perhaps, was the confidence that there were others, a lot of others, who had no doubt about an ordinary working woman's right to go about in public, unmolested.

There must have been any number of less reassuring stories in the Mumbai of that time and in the decades that followed, but the city was, and is, relatively friendly to its women. *Relatively* is important, I learnt, when I moved, after years in Mumbai and Chennai, to Delhi.

In the early '80s, there was no metro in Delhi, and I had to change two buses to get to work. At this point in my life, I must have looked like a caricature of respectable Indian womanhood, my starched cotton sari wrapped modestly round a visibly pregnant body. But being a monument-in-the-making to that great Indian temple, motherhood, did not make a difference to the fact that I was a woman in Delhi. A woman with a body, alone in a crowded bus. I learnt the basic survival tactics, the handbag hanging behind to protect my back, safety pins on hips, that sort of thing. But still it meant being cautious about where you went and who you went with. It meant worrying about getting a lift back if you were out at night. It meant being aware, a good part of your waking day, that you are a *woman*, and that at any minute, anywhere, the abrasive city would turn on you through one of its ordinary citizens who had turned into a male predator.

Delhi, of course, does not hold a monopoly on male predators. Indeed, a quick reference to the anti-women state of the world may be a good idea to pre-empt any smug and easy "Western us versus Eastern them". Like the rest of the world then, India has its own versions of keeping women well within real and imaginary lines. There are instances of harassment of women, various forms of violence against women, in any Indian city or village. The lower down on the class or caste or community scale, the more vulnerable the woman. But Delhi—the large area now called the National Capital Region—seems to have taken upon itself the symbol of everything in India that is determined to treat its women as unequal citizens. It seems astonishing, and admirable, that the city's women have not grown paranoid over the years; that they still go about their work and their lives; that they still partake of what the city has to offer, and fight for their right to do precisely that.

On a Sunday evening in December 2012, a young woman and a male friend went to see *The Life of Pi* in a mall in the Saket area of South Delhi. (In one of those ironies our lives are made of, *saket* means heaven; it is also an ancient name of Ayodhya, the place that is believed, to the considerable cost of present day Indians, to be the birthplace of Rama.) The 23-year-old woman was a physiotherapy student, the bright spark in her family. Her father moved to Delhi from his ancestral village in the early '80s, and after a long struggle to make a life for his family in the capital, now worked as a baggage loader in the airport.

On their way back from the mall, the couple got into a bus. The bus turned out to be the kind of unlicensed bus that can run in Delhi after paying a few bribes. Much worse, the bus had five men, including the driver, who were, in their words, "looking for fun", having already robbed a passenger and thrown him off the vehicle. What followed was an unbelievably brutal gang rape of the young woman, which left her with part of her intestines hanging out. Both she and her injured friend were thrown off the bus onto a road. They lay there bleeding, naked, for 45 minutes before the police arrived and the woman was taken to hospital.

No city, least of all Delhi, is a stranger to all kinds of violence against women. But this time, the city erupted. The crowd gathered outside the Safdarjang Hospital where the woman was fighting for her life. So did the media. Students distributed candles and we lit them, silent for the most part. There was a strange combination of disbelief, fear and anger in the air.

In the heart of the city, in the heart of its map of power—Parliament House, Raisina Hill, Rashtrapati Bhawan, India Gate, Rajpath and Janpath, Jantar Mantar—it was mostly anger that drove large numbers on to the streets, from old women to school children. In the first couple of days, many who had been marching for years for women's rights were stunned—as were the police—by the numbers, the baby-faced girls screaming with determination, "*We want justice!*"

Inevitably, the numbers swelled with the usual suspects and their accompanying crowds: politicians and aspiring politicians, "godmen", several right-wing groups not exactly known for their devotion to the progress of women. Everyone was outraged, but the "solutions" were hotly contested. Would hanging the rapists be a "deterrent" when the statistics showed so many instances of sexual assault by members of the family or the neighbourhood? Did "protecting" women mean policing them more, literally and otherwise? Was this brutality evidence of patriarchy in general? Of urbanisation? Globalisation?

There is no doubt that in the new India, obsessed with its growth story, people have been marginalised in ways that just may help turn men into beasts that roam rural and urban jungles, looking for prey, taking out their free-floating frustration on them. But this sort of brutal-system-turning-men-brutal "explanation" was simply not enough for the angry and shaken women of Delhi. While the crowds gathered on the streets, and the authorities shut down some metro stations and pulled out their water cannons and lathis and tear gas to bring back "law and order", all kinds of people spoke on television and in public meetings, or wrote in newspapers and on the net. The government finally woke up and set up a committee, the Verma Committee, to process a range of suggestions and make recommendations. The Committee did its job; it stretched Delhi to India, examined the entire landscape, from the meanings and categories of sexual harassment, to the effect of militarisation on women in places like Kashmir and the North East.

Meanwhile, the anguished public debate continued. And as always, the debate engendered a counter "debate" in which public figures, politicians, self-proclaimed godmen and respectable members of the public either blamed the "victims" in some way; or screamed for capital punishment as a deterrent; or asked for more protection—read policing—of women in public spaces; or a return from wicked modern ways to good old traditional India, where, apparently, rapes, by gangs or otherwise, were unheard of.

Not many of these newfound experts on Indian women championed the more path-breaking recommendations of the Verma Committee. To acknowledge that violence against women is part of a larger societal problem, to talk of marital rape, or of what caste, class or militarisation does every day to women, was more than these people, or indeed the government, could handle. "Closure", that trendy new solution to all problems, was achieved by a court that gave the rapists (except the juvenile offender) death sentences. And to let us know that the world that made the rape possible is still intact, the defence lawyer of the rapists declared to the media that if he had a daughter who went out with a young man at night, or had premarital sex with him, he would burn her alive.

Between the '80s when I moved to Delhi and now, judicial activism in general, and the efforts of women's organisations in particular, have worked hard to make the city a better place for its women. They have worked in the courts and in Parliament; they have worked through contact with women and through protest on the streets. Women's organisations have led protests against a range of horrors: dowry deaths; domestic violence; sexual harassment at the workplace; the frequent "caste atrocity", the least atrocious of these involving women stripped and paraded naked as a lesson to their men; rape and its subset, gang rape; and increasingly, as if to tie all these forms of violence together into a bizarre twist of ugly logic, "honour" killings.

Maybe these honour crimes hold, in some way, and to some extent, a key to making a little more sense of the continuing and new forms of violence against women. Haryana, next door to Delhi, has one of the worst sex ratios in the country. It is also one of the places where the writ of the *khap panchayat* [a gathering of village elders—*Ed.*]—the "traditional" and unofficial caste *panchayat*—runs rampant. Despite the industrialisation and "modernisation" of states like Haryana, the *khap*, a cluster of villages united by caste and geography, thrives; and so do *khap panchayat*s, feudal bodies set up to settle local disputes in the absence of law enforcement agencies. *Khap panchayat*s are undemocratic—their members and leaders are not elected, and they are tyrannical about imposing their "rules". They are particularly repressive toward women. The honour of the caste is seen to be vested in the "chastity" of women. They oppose equal rights for women in property, are against co-ed schools, support dress codes for women, and oppose women's rights to divorce and widow re-marriage. "Youth wings" of unemployed and lumpen men have been formed to "protect old customs and traditions by all means".

The violent ethos bred by *khap panchayat*s show how, in the name of "tradition", existing power structures, unofficial or official, perform new tricks to exert control on women, dalits, Muslims, youth. Girls and boys are to follow the "rules" about who they may befriend or marry. If these rules are broken, the result could be murder, "honour suicides", threat and intimidation, fines, economic and social boycott of the offenders and their families. Despite a veneer of modernisation, the guiding principle is caste. The *khap panchayat*s aggressively push a worldview in which caste divisions are desirable; and violence against other castes, through their women, routine. Such is the power of the "*khap panchayat* mentality" that the recent surge in the number of reported rapes against Dalit girls has not got the kind of police, state, media or public attention they should.

A kind of *khap panchayat* mentality seems to have spread to Delhi, city of new and old outsiders. Such a mentality feeds into the existing power set-up, and allows for brutal violence against women to keep them in control. This may serve as one possible context to "understand" the bus gang rape in Delhi, and the numerous cases of sexual assault that continue to be reported—and unreported.

Women in Delhi have long lived in a state of low-grade siege. It's just that it's out in the open now, no longer an urban legend that only women know to be true. My hope has always been in the women's organisations that have worked hard and long to end this siege. But now, after the reaction to the December gang rape [2012], I also see hope in the energy unleashed by the thousands of girls and women on the streets. As we laid siege to the presidential Rashtrapati Bhawan, young voices rending the air with their demand for justice, I recall wondering, 'Do they know what a city-changing, life-changing thing they are asking for?'

I would like to think this energy will grow, one day at a time, into something strong and thoughtful, so we will re-learn what it is, this justice being demanded. We may then build a New Delhi.

Voices for the Voiceless—Transforming Women's Lives in Rural India

Armene Modi

Armene Modi has received multiple awards and honours—including a CNN-IBN Real Heroes Award, and in 2016, a Rotarians Literacy Hero Award—for her work to improve the quality of life in rural India, especially for village women. How she came to this task, and what she did, are recounted here in her own words.

"A journey of a thousand miles begins with the first step", an ancient proverb states. My journey from Tokyo, Japan, to the remote villages of Shirur County in Pune District was inspired by Gandhi's oft-quoted message: "Be the change you want to see in the world." It began in 1997 with the chance reading of a book by Elisabeth Bumiller titled *May You Be the Mother of a 100 Sons: A Journey among the Women of India* (1990). A simple statistic in the book, that according to the 1991 census, 61% of Indian women were still illiterate, shocked me deeply. It spoke volumes about the condition of women, particularly marginalised women, in India in the 1990s. Literacy would clearly be a powerful tool to help create a better tomorrow for those in India who were poor and female.

I was in my tenth year of a personally satisfying career teaching English at a well-known university in Japan. A course on Peace Education led me to integrate peace and human rights learning into my English language courses. The response from students was tremendous and many were motivated to campaign for various human rights issues. For my part, I often felt guilty that while I was motivating my students to take action, I myself was not really doing anything to make a difference. That statistic about female illiteracy in India was like a wake-up call that shook me out of my complacency. I felt that as an educator, my skills were perhaps needed more back home than in Japan. And that is how Ashta No Kai (ANK), a women's literacy and development project, was born—with the aim of educating and empowering marginalised women in India.

As a first step, I wrote a one-page proposal to set up a small project in a local slum near my mother's home in Pune. When I circulated it among friends and colleagues in Japan, the response was, much to my great surprise, overwhelming. My campaign plea that literacy could change the cycle of poverty and dependence which characterised the lives of poor women touched a chord among many Japanese. The idea of a slum school was reminiscent of the *terakoya* elementary schools in Japan's Edo period in the 19th century, temple schools for commoners which had helped ordinary Japanese achieve a high level of literacy. As a result, more than one thousand Japanese friends, colleagues and acquaintances sympathetic to the cause pledged their wholehearted support. Before long five groups—in Shizuoka Prefecture, Kawasaki city, Sumida-ku (a ward of Tokyo), cities on the island of Kyushu, and a student group at J.F. Oberlin University—formed an umbrella organisation: Ashta No Kai-Japan. The project seemed to have taken on a life of its own.

With such resounding support, it was impossible to limit ANK's work to just one slum in Pune. The reach had to be wider. During one of my trips to Pune, I had the good fortune to meet a renowned surgeon and social activist Dr. Banoo Coyaji. Her NGO, the KEM Hospital Research Centre, had a health project in thirty villages in Shirur County. Dr. Coyaji suggested that ANK's work would be more effective if it were rural-based, as the need for such an intervention was much greater in the villages. She kindly offered to assist in setting up the project, which was a great boon as I had no experience in the social sector field. I was also very struck with a quotation of India's first Prime Minister, Jawaharlal Nehru, that was prominently displayed in her office: "To awaken people, it is the woman who must be awakened. Once she is on the move, the family moves, the village moves, the nation moves." It was as if fate itself had led me there.

ANK was formally launched on October 9th, 1998, with 23 Japanese supporters who had come to Pune especially to attend the opening ceremony. Ten drought-prone villages and hamlets located in the interior of Shirur County at a distance of about 55 to 70 kilometres from Pune were selected as the project area. The villages, with an approximate total population of 15,000, lacked such basic infrastructure as adequate schools, clean water supply, health care facilities, toilets, electricity, and good roads. A typical village consisted of a central cluster of houses, surrounded by many satellite hamlet settlements, which were two to five kilometres away. Access to many hamlets was difficult due to lack of transportation and bad roads. As in many parts of the country, the status of women in Shirur County too was low. Poverty, ignorance, illiteracy, and rigid social traditions hampered women's progress and affected the quality of their lives.

A major challenge ANK faced during its inception was the promotion and achievement of literacy among adult women. An initial survey conducted in 1999 in the project area revealed that there was a high level of illiteracy among the women, 54% as compared with 23% among the men. Fourteen literacy centres were set up in the target villages with the hope that the campaign slogan of 100% literacy would soon become a reality. I was in for a rude shock. Even after two years of struggling to promote literacy, the programme benefited only a handful of women. The top-down approach of assuming that literacy was what rural women needed had not worked. To be sure, individual women realised the long-term benefits, but their need for literacy paled in comparison to the immediate necessities of their daily life. What women wanted were income-generating activities and access to credit.

Fortunately, around the same time, the Self-Help Group movement (SHGs) was taking off in India. The reality on the ground dictated that ANK too should begin to organise women into these micro-credit models of voluntary savings and loan collectives. Hundred twenty-five Self-Help Groups were soon established in ten villages to enable rural women to access funds for emergencies and undertake income-generating activities. SHGs proved to be a great boon to poor women. Despite having no collateral as individuals, they were now able to access credit to undertake income-generating activities by collectively pooling whatever little savings they had, and, most importantly, escape the clutches of moneylenders who charged as much as 120% interest.

SHGs initiated a silent revolution in the villages. Thanks to SHGs, more than 3,000 women were helped to personal empowerment and some degree of financial independence. It is important to point out that ANK merely acted as a catalyst in setting them up. All decisions regarding the SHGs were made by the women themselves; from the selection of members and office bearers, the meeting dates, monthly saving targets, and loan disbursement, to the amount of interest to be charged and the repayment schedules. Poor and illiterate women now began to make decisions that affected their lives, gaining individual strength and confidence as part of a group in the bargain.

Today the SHGs are run entirely by village women and act as a backbone for the majority of village activities. Women who had hitherto never left the four walls of their homes except to fetch water have realised their strength in unity. They band together to solve the problems of their village, whether it is banning illicit liquor sale in the village, improving the poor quality of the school's midday meal, dealing with absentee teachers, or even coping with infrastructural problems like water shortages and bad roads. Village women successfully run dairy cooperatives as well, and manage 200 backyard poultry projects. The approximately 5,000 USD a month that the dairy cooperatives bring in are a welcome addition to the village income of many families.

Believing sanitation to be a human right, ANK decided to tackle the situation of open defecation in ANK villages in 2008. A large number of village homes in the ANK target area had no toilets. Open defecation was still widely practised in the villages. An area within the home was cordoned off for washing and bathing but no space was allocated for a toilet. Although some of the wealthier villagers had built toilets perhaps as a status symbol, the poor had no other option but to use the outdoors as a toilet. The hygiene situation in the villages was further exacerbated by the scarcity of water, leaving much to be desired in terms of personal hygiene.

The lack of toilets was particularly hard on women in ANK's villages, making daily life for them an even greater struggle. The need for privacy often forced many of them to walk long distances and relieve themselves only before sunrise or after sunset. It was even worse for expectant mothers and mothers who had just given birth. Other difficulties that women encountered while defecating in the open were adverse weather conditions and the danger posed by wild animals. There were several known cases in the villages of women getting severe injuries due to such attacks, which cost them dearly in medical bills. Worse, there was also the fear of sexual harassment and assault, even rape, when a woman ventured out alone. For the above reasons, many women were afraid to go to the toilet in the outdoors but had no other option. The menfolk had no qualms about using public spaces to relieve themselves, but the need for privacy at such times for women was essential to their well-being.

Until recently, there were no toilets in the schools in ANK villages either. Children were forced to use the surrounding open ground, resulting in a lack of privacy and in highly unsanitary conditions. This posed an even greater problem for adolescent girls in particular. Some of them dropped out of the school system in higher grades, due to this lack.

ANK decided to build 80 toilets for poor women in one of its villages as a pilot project, hoping that this would largely improve the sanitation situation in the village. The Ecosan toilet, promoted by UNICEF as an effective model for promoting long-term sustainable sanitation, was introduced in Nimgaon Bhogi village. Its eco-friendly design broke up human excreta into a dehydrated, odourless compost-like material using a natural biological process. It was particularly useful in water-scarce areas, as it needed only about three litres of water as compared to 12 to 15 litres for a conventional toilet. The experiment, however, proved to be a failure. Despite having a toilet at their doorstep, people still preferred to defecate in the open. The biggest hurdle in implementing the sanitation project was the difficulty in challenging age-old traditions, conservative rural mindsets and in convincing people to change their age-old habits.

When the literacy programme for adult women did not prove to be very effective, ANK decided to turn its attention to decreasing the dropout rate for girls, believing that the educated girl of today would become the empowered woman of tomorrow. Educated girls were more likely to resist pressures to marry too young or have too many children, and would be better mothers. Educating girls was a major challenge for ANK, since in 2000 there was only one local high school, which was four to eight kilometres away from the ten villages that ANK was working in. Parents fearful for their daughters' safety and sceptical of the benefits of educating them did not normally encourage the girls to attend high school. Instead, girls as young as 13 and 14 were simply being married off.

To improve the access of village girls to higher education and to address the social problem of child marriages, I decided to launch a Bicycle Bank in 2001, an innovative initiative at the time. Village girls were given bicycles to attend high school, since most of them lived over four or more kilometres away from the school, a fact which resulted in the high dropout rate. The bicycles proved to be wheels of change that impacted the lives of hundreds of girls. To date, ANK's Bicycle Bank has enabled 1,000 girls to stay on in school. Girls' attendance in schools is at almost 100%; in fact, in some village high schools there are now more girls than boys in the classroom. More importantly, fewer village girls are now married off before the legal age of 18. The positive impact of the Bicycle Bank was noted in 2014 when ANK ran short of funding for the project. Surprisingly, not a single girl dropped out, and every girl from Grade 7 went on to Grade 8. Oftentimes, one is pleasantly surprised at such unintended outcomes of projects.

A natural offshoot of the Bicycle Bank project was a scholarship programme that was launched in 2004 and which has, so far, provided 950 girls with scholarships to pursue higher education. From the nine girls who applied in 2004, the number of applicants each year is around 100 and increasing. With the aspirational level rising, rural girls are now pursuing higher studies and venturing into fields like dentistry, computer science, electronics, engineering, automobile engineering and pharmacy, besides the more traditional ones. It is very encouraging to note that many rural girls are now able to avail themselves of opportunities that their mothers and grandmothers could never have dreamed of.

Another initiative for adolescent girls, *Kishori Mandal*s, was launched in 2001. Weekly meetings conducted by empowered grassroots workers raised awareness of gender issues, including laws relating to evil customs like dowry and early marriages, and gave rural girls critical inputs in life skills. The meetings provided a platform for the girls to build their self-confidence and independence. Recognising that women empowerment and equality cannot be achieved through the efforts of women alone and that it requires male support and behaviour change among men as well, ANK recently initiated weekly workshops to help adolescent boys understand the importance of these issues. *Kishor Mandal*s were initiated in 2012 to help adolescent boys, who are at an impressionable age, question traditional male stereotypes in society and work on changing their own attitudes so as to promote a more gender-equitable society in village communities.

India has recently seen a sharp rise in the number of rapes and sexual crimes against women and children, as is evident from recent horrific cases that have been in the news. The rape of a young medical student on a Delhi bus in December 2012 shamed India and shocked the world. With increasing incidents of violence against women, I decided to introduce karate classes for the girls, the *kishoris*, in 2012 to help them combat increasing gender-based violence, and arm them with the skills they needed to stay healthy and live free from violence. Besides this, karate would instill discipline and self-confidence in them, knowing that they could protect themselves if attacked.

One of the greatest challenges that ANK has continued to face is gender discrimination born of a deep-rooted patriarchal mindset, making it difficult to convince rural people to transform their traditional ways of thinking and overcome gender bias. The road ahead for rural women to achieve both social and economic equality in India is still long and arduous. Men largely continue to make major family decisions, while women keep on bearing the burden of household chores. Worse, rural women buy into gender stereotypes, accepting and even justifying domestic violence without question, as they feel that a woman's role is to be submissive. In addition, women have little control over their own fertility and reproductive health due to the strong preference for a son. Moreover, with little awareness of their legal rights, women are routinely discriminated against in land and property rights too.

Despite the gender inequity that poor rural women face on a daily basis, ANK has made great efforts to help them make a better world for themselves. It has supported women empowerment efforts and addressed their multi-dimensional needs by giving them access to work and income, to information, and to opportunities and choices. The combination of added financial autonomy and increased confidence levels has given rural women a significant voice in their communities. They are now viewed as assets rather than liabilities and have begun to negotiate new roles and opportunities for themselves. Women have begun to participate in village governance and development and have started demanding their rights to public services and goods. It is encouraging to see poor women who were once powerless gain a greater sense of security, a greater sense of dignity, a greater sense of self-worth, and a vision of the future. Most importantly, there is a positive change in their social status. They command greater respect within their households and extended families.

Ashta No Kai was established in 1998 to bring hope, strength and a chance of empowerment to marginalised women. Seventeen years later, it is watching the seeds it planted grow, knowing that it has made a positive difference to the lives of the many women and girls it has touched. Rural women have been deeply influenced by ANK's commitment to education, literacy, financial independence, and social justice. The NGO has acted as a catalyst for social change by raising women's consciousness about gender inequalities, has helped them to identify and analyse some of the critical issues and problems they face in their lives, and has given them the confidence to find and seek their own solutions.

I have never regretted the decision to retire from teaching and re-invent myself as a social activist. Although the work in the field has involved many challenges, it has been a rich journey of discovery and learning. I have felt truly humbled to observe how cheerful and content the women are despite the little they have. I admire their courage and fortitude, their resilience, endurance and strength despite their struggle for survival working against incredible odds of poverty, victimisation, vulnerability and exploitation. It is encouraging to know that ANK's efforts towards empowering rural women have resulted in their finding a voice and a platform to participate actively in their own development. The project has been effective in enabling many rural women to achieve their full potential as literate, healthy, skilled and socially aware individuals. There is still, however, much work to be done. I look forward to a day when a world of gender inequality, poverty, violence and injustice will be replaced by a world where women and men work together as allies to build a culture of peace, in which Gandhi's dream of "wiping the tear from every eye" can finally become a reality.

Gay in India?

R. Raj Rao

R. Raj Rao, poet, playwright, novelist, critic and biographer, Professor of English at Pune University, and gay rights activist, is also the author of a lively weekly newspaper column in the Pune Mirror, *"Man to Man". The following selection of articles takes a look at what it means to be gay in India, with a chilling glance at how another country, Nazi Germany, dealt with its "homophiles".*

BAD NEWS

While mainstream India rejoices over the election results and the formation of the new government, the verdict doesn't augur well for the queer community. We are full of apprehension. Will we be treated on a par with other social and political criminals? Will there be witch-hunts to get us?

When the Supreme Court upturned the Delhi High Court ruling of July 2009, which de-criminalised consensual gay sex among adults by reading down Section 377 of the Indian Penal Code, it put the onus on the Government of India, saying it was for the government to amend the existing law if it thought fit. That, of course, would depend on which government was in power.

From the way Sonia Gandhi and Rahul Gandhi reacted to the judgement, making it clear they were outraged by it because it was an intrusion of privacy, we knew that the Congress, if it came to power, would initiate steps to change the law. Later, Kejriwal's Aam Aadmi Party also held meetings with queer activists, reiterating that they were appalled by the judgement and would do everything they could to restore the fundamental rights of gay people. That is why, the "wave" notwithstanding, most gay men and women, I am told, voted for the Congress and the Aam Aadmi Party.

The BJP, however, was jubilant about the judgement from the very start. It supported it *in toto*, which meant that they would do nothing to introduce a parliamentary amendment that led to the scrapping of Section 377. It was obvious why the BJP took such a stand. As a Hindu nationalist party, it believed it had to safeguard Indian culture and Indian values, and homosexuality, according to it, was against Indian culture. The people of India did not want it. According to the BJP, homosexuality is a Western fad that touches the lives of a few phony upper-class Indians, while middle-class India knows not the ABC of it. What middle-class India knows is heterosexuality, marriage, procreation and the starting of family, made up of father, mother, brother and sister. And Section 377 of the Indian Penal Code endorses all that.

But this brings me to the other worrying thing—the thing about minorities. The party that won the mandate of the junta is known to be myopic about the existence of minorities. Their hostility towards religious minorities, especially Muslims, is legion. If they believe that homosexuals are also a minority—I am not sure about this, given that many Indian men have had sex with other men at least once in their life—it means that we are invisible to our government, we do not exist for them, we are our country's lost property, as the poet Adil Jussawalla once wrote in a poem, albeit in a different context.

When the Supreme Court delivered its judgement on Section 377 in December last year, it capitalised on the word "minority". It suggested that a law that was in place for 143 years did not have to change to suit the whims and fancies of a miniscule [*sic*] minority. It was as if the judiciary was colluding with the legislature here to blot out the presence of minorities. That left only the executive, the babus of babuland, the police included, who are not exactly known to be the best friends of gay folk.

The election results have veritably pushed the gay community against a wall. First, the December 2013 judgement wasn't in our favour. Then, a review petition that was filed to reconsider the December judgement was dismissed by the Supreme Court. A curative petition that was subsequently filed to review the December judgement again shows no signs of coming up for hearing. And now, a political party that is vociferously opposed to legitimising non-heterosexual sex gets a thumping majority in Parliament.

In the bargain, there's only one thing we can wish for. It is that the drug cartels should research a pill that when popped with a glass of water like, say, an aspirin tablet instantly reverses our sexuality, converting all homosexual men and women into heterosexuals overnight. It's the only way we can become visible, and the chemists are likely to make huge profits.

DOUBLE STANDARDS

So the Supreme Court has recognised transgender as the third gender, neither male nor female. This is terrific. However, the judgement runs contradictory to the apex court's judgement of December 11th, 2013, which re-criminalised homosexuality. Transgender people are never heterosexual. The conflict between their biological and psychological identities ensures that they are sexually attracted to people of their own sex. A transgender male, for example, *feels* that he is a woman, partly because he is sexually attracted to men. The Supreme Court is spot on when it says that transgender people deserve the same rights as others. It is also laudable that it recommends reservations for them in educational institutions and government jobs. From now on, we're likely to see another abbreviation, TG, in addition to the existing SC, ST, OBC, *etc.*, in newspaper classifieds. I will return to the issue of reservations later. But first, let me address the issue of sex.

"Carnal intercourse" (or anal sex) is right now illegal, an offence punishable under Section 377 of the Indian Penal Code. However, the new Supreme Court judgement excludes transgender people from the provisions of the section. What this means is that if a gay man has "unnatural" sex with a transgender male (and many transgender males do sex work for a living), the gay man alone will be punished. This is absurd because it violates the principle of equality before the law.

It's a Catch 22 situation. If the court upheld transgender rights but continued to criminalise (or at least remain silent about) their sexual behaviour, it would imply that transgender people must remain celibate for the rest of their lives!

Ideally, the two cases, the appeal against the Delhi High Court ruling that read down Section 377, and the PIL filed by the NGO Alliance India for transgender rights, should have been heard together by the same bench. The hands of the present bench, comprising Justices K.S. Radhakrishnan and A.K. Sikri, were obviously tied. They couldn't embarrass the Supreme Court by going against its own (December 11th) judgement. Hence, they made it clear that "While dealing with the present issue, we are not concerned with this aforesaid wider meaning of the expression transgender." The "aforesaid wider meaning" has of course to do with the clubbing together of lesbian, gay and bisexual with transgender, represented by the popular abbreviation LGBT. This drives a wedge within the queer community, leading to resentment.

The funniest part, however, is that the law now has a serious loophole. There is no acid test to prove that one is a transgender. Castration could be a criterion, but then as Salman Rushdie reveals in the book *AIDS Sutra* (Akhavi 2008, 111) only about 60% of Bombay's *hijras* (male-to-female transgender individuals) are castrated. Castration is a painful operation. The writer John Irving graphically describes it in his novel *A Son of the Circus* (1994):

> The surgeon (who is not a surgeon) ties a string around the penis and the testicles in order to get a clean cut—for it is with one cut that both the penis and the testicles are removed. The patient is allowed to bleed freely; it's believed that maleness is a kind of poison, purged by bleeding (58).

Thus, homosexual men, often naturally effeminate, could (should) take advantage of the law by playing up their camp behaviour and claiming to be transgender. All it would take on their part is to cross-dress (or dress in drag), walk coquettishly, pierce their ear, nose or eyebrow, and cultivate feminine body language. It is downmarket homosexuals (like *kotis*, effeminate men who take on the passive role in same-sex relations), rather than well-heeled ones, who are more likely to benefit from this loophole in the law, because transgender people are somehow associated with poverty and illiteracy, though that is not always the case. Farah Rustom and Aida Banaji (about whom the late Riyad Wadia made a documentary) were well-known transgender people who later became transsexuals. Both were well-off and well-educated.

As for job reservations, the judgement opens up a Pandora's Box. "Transgender" is a psychological state, difficult to prove by clinical means. Homosexual men who are not transgender can easily lay claim to jobs reserved for the latter, citing merely their sexual orientation as proof. Sexual orientation, being biological, is, after all, relatively easier to prove. The rest, as explained above, can be simulated. Such misuse of the law isn't new. Heterosexual men in developing countries are habitually known to claim that they're homosexual, in order to get "asylum" in developed countries like the United States.

Look what a tangle the Supreme Court has landed itself in.

TRUE COLOURS

Predictably, the Government of India has done what we expected it to do. It has challenged the Supreme Court's April 2014 judgement on transgender rights, proving, in the bargain, that it cares a farthing for judicial independence. Clearly, the affinities of the government lie instead with the retrograde apex court judgement of December 2013 that restored the status quo on Section 377 of the Indian Penal Code. That status quo lay dismantled for a brief four-and-a-half-year period of sunshine, owing to the Delhi High Court's reading down of that archaic law, introduced by Lord Macaulay in 1869.

The Attorney General, it seems, hasn't even bothered to read the April 2014 judgement carefully. That is why one of his contentions is that lesbian, gay and bisexual sexual identities must be de-linked from transgender identities. But that is exactly what the Supreme Court did, or was obliged to do, because it couldn't contradict its own judgement of December 2013 that re-criminalised homosexuality. The bench that authored the latter judgement was evidently of a progressive mindset, unlike the bench that authored the earlier judgement. It cleverly found a loophole in the law when it upheld transgender rights, because in the alphabet cocktail of L, G, B and T, the T alone has to do with gender identity, while the other letters have to do with sexual preference. Thus, the government makes a serious mistake when it assumes that "transgender" is an umbrella term that also covers lesbian, gay and bisexual identities.

However, as I have pointed out in a previous column, and as a recent edit page article in a national daily argues, there are overlaps between transgender on the one hand, and lesbian, gay and bisexual on the other, that make the April 2014 judgement somewhat untenable. If a transgendered person is also gay, it is ridiculous to say that the former person in him has rights, while the latter person does not.

The April 2014 judgement spoke of giving OBC status to transgenders, which would entitle them to government jobs through the quota system. Our homophobic government takes exception to that as well, bringing in a technicality. OBC status, it claims, cannot be given to transgenders, in spite of the Supreme Court ruling, because that would have to be okayed first by the National Commission for Backward Classes (NCBC). Needless to say, the NCBC, already an overcrowded steamboat, is not going to okay it. In India, the *hijras* are the most visible face of transgendered people, and everyone knows that the only work they are able to find is singing and dancing, and selling their bodies, all for a pittance. Reserving government jobs for them would perhaps enable them to lead dignified lives, but who says the government cares about their dignity?

When, on that black day in December 2013, the Supreme Court declared homosexual sex in India to be illegal, even if it was consensual and involved adults (persons above the age of eighteen), the BJP was effectively the only political party that lauded the judgement. At that time, of course, it was still not in power at the centre. Today it is. And we can see through its filibuster tactics when it tells the court that it cannot implement its recommendations in six months, as that is too short a time. We can also gauge its arrogance and its utter disregard for the independence of the judiciary when it talks of constituting its own panel and going strictly by their recommendations.

A section of the media has advised the government to amend India's anti-gay law once and for all, because now, apart from a curative petition that is supposed to come up for hearing in the Supreme Court, and that by a larger bench, it is the Government of India alone that can come to the rescue of its queer population. These newspapers and TV channels tell the government that it can safely afford to lose some of the votes of its conservative, right-wing voters, in exchange for the laurels it would earn from the international community for jettisoning one of its most discriminatory laws. But is the government in a mood to take heed? If anything, since May this year [2014] and now, it has only revealed its true colours, given the anti-minority soups it lands itself in almost every day. To this government, sexual minorities, like religious minorities, need to be shown their place.

HISTORY LESSON

Homosexuality is not unique to mankind. It exists among animals, birds and insects as well. The National Geographic channel frequently airs a programme that shows animals indulging in gay behaviour. My favourite part comes when the camera zooms in on a pair of lesbian lizards.

As far as human beings are concerned, homosexuality was practised by the ancient Greeks and Romans. But it wasn't called homosexuality then. It was called sodomy, and it had to do not just with pleasure but also with power. The sodomite or penetrator in ancient Greece and Rome was a man who was free. The sodomised or penetrated, on the other hand, was a boy who was a slave. Only the slave could be penetrated. If a free man was penetrated, it was thought to be immoral.

Homosexuality was also known (and practised) in ancient and pre-colonial India. The one text that proves this is of course the *Kamasutra*. The *Kamasutra* obviously does not use words like homosexual or gay, but it frequently refers to the "third sex", meaning those who are neither male nor female. Then there's Khajuraho in Madhya Pradesh, where most of the sculpture on the temple walls depicts orgies in which both men and women participate. This wouldn't be the case if heterosexuality was the only sexuality that the people of that time knew. In addition, there are homosexual myths and legends, many of them involving our gods, goddesses and saints.

In colonial India, two poetic forms are supposed to have been distinctly gay. One was the *ghazal*, where men wrote love lyrics to men. The other was *rekhti* poetry, where men assumed the personae of women and wrote erotic verse to them.

All this is encapsulated in an illuminating book titled *Same-Sex Love in India* (2000), edited by Ruth Vanita and Saleem Kidwai. At first, no Indian publisher dared to publish the book, thinking it to be controversial, and the authors approached an American publisher to bring it out. Seeing its success, however, the Indian publishing industry relented and brought out Indian editions of it that can today be had for less than five hundred rupees.

The terms "homosexual" and "heterosexual" first made their appearance in the 19th century, and ironically, the former term preceded the latter. This means that heterosexuality was being understood in terms of homosexuality, and not the other way round. The British ruled us by then, and foisted their quaint morality on us. Anything to do with sex scandalised the Victorians of the 19th century, and they bequeathed that mindset to Indians. In the 20th century, the majority of Indians were inheritors of that mindset, making all sex talk taboo. That we have a poor sense of history only contributed to our amnesia (or loss of memory) that made us forget the *Kamasutra* and Khajuraho. Indians don't read the *Kamasutra* anymore, and most of us don't even know where Khajuraho is.

It is strange that people across the spectrum, from politicians, corporate managers and bureaucrats to the common man who travels in jam-packed trains and buses, should think that homosexuality is against Indian culture. It is this ignorance that gave a boost to the recent Supreme Court judgement that re-criminalised homosexuality in India all over again, after a four-year reprieve that it got when the Delhi High Court de-criminalised it. As everyone knows, there was a famous (notorious?) yoga guru at the centre of the appeal, and the Supreme Court thought that he represented the pulse of India when he argued that if homosexuality were legalised, the next we would want would be the legalisation of bestiality.

What we ought to realise, however, is that our myopic view of history only makes the Victorians successful in their endeavour to erase our past, which they thought was worthless. And this wasn't just about our sexual past. It was also about our linguistic past, as English replaced Sanskrit. Significantly, it was the same man, T.B. Macaulay, who was behind both these moves, and his initials always strike me as a hint that he was sick.

Victorian morality embarrassed the English of the 20th century, who distanced themselves from it. Today, England, like America and the rest of Europe, is fairly permissive, and homosexuality isn't outlawed there. We, in contrast, were so enamoured of the Victorians that we continue to cling on to their beliefs.

UNHOLY TRINITY

Homosexuality has always been looked upon with disfavour by three agencies universal to mankind.

The first of these is *religion*. Although attitudes to deviant desire vary from religion to religion, with some religions like Hinduism being less judgemental about it than others like Islam and Christianity, religions, on the whole, believe that the purpose of human sexuality is procreation, which keeps the life cycle going. To religion, sexual activity is a means to an end, not an end in itself. To foreground the recreational aspect of sex, which, in a sense, is what homosexuality does, is to treat sex as an end in itself, as perhaps the animals do. But man, who has been gifted with reason, cannot afford to be like the animals. He must manage his sexual life responsibly, and he can only be said to do so, when he practises procreative sex. Now, heterosexual sex alone is procreative, and even though heterosexuals do not always have sex to reproduce, heterosexuality must be given the benefit of the doubt. By contrast, homosexual sex can never be procreative, unless science intervenes and makes this possible. But scientific inventions have rarely curried favour with religion that is orthodox by definition. If science makes it possible for a man to get pregnant, we can be sure that religions, across the spectrum, rather than laud the achievement will see it as the handiwork of the Devil.

Then there's *the law*. In Plato's ideal republic, human beings are so wise that they do not need laws to govern them, but laws exist everywhere else in the world. And the law, somehow, has always thought of homosexuals as outlaws, perhaps because they cannot become in-laws. That is to say, if homosexuals are attracted to their own sex, they will not get married, and if they don't marry, they will not have fathers-in-law and mothers-in-law, and in turn will not be sons-in-law and daughters-in-law. In the West, laws have had to be amended to accommodate homosexuals—it's not as if they did not exist in the first place. In the East, laws differ from country to country, with some Muslim countries still having laws in their law books that make it mandatory for homosexuals to be stoned to death. In India, we aren't that bad, but then, as we all know, there's the notorious Section 377 of the Indian Penal Code that makes homosexual activity a criminal offence. Everywhere in the world, anti-gay laws have given the police, who are enforcers of the law, *carte blanche* to harass homosexuals, and the harassment may vary from blackmail and extortion to gay bashing that can even lead to death. In the 20th century, such homophobic atrocities have been reported from countries as diverse as Iran on the one hand and America on the other.

Finally, there's *medicine*. Medicine, with its overemphasis on the biological, has always pathologised homosexuality, taking it to be a disorder. Like religion, medicine disapproves of homosexuality because it thinks it to be against nature's design, which is to ensure that the species reproduce till they become extinct. In America, it took a good deal of brainwashing by gay activists to get the American Psychiatric Association to knock homosexuality off its list of mental disorders. But hardly had they succeeded when AIDS made its appearance and got the medical fraternity hyper once again. Doctors saw AIDS as a gay disease, and some even went on to suggest that AIDS, with its painful symptoms, was the punishment meted out to homosexuals for sinful sexual behaviour. In turn, many homosexual men became subscribers to a "conspiracy theory" that held that AIDS was a cunning invention of doctors and chemists who wanted to foist expensive medicines manufactured by multinational drug cartels on unsuspecting homosexuals with seemingly huge disposable incomes. For in those early days, AIDS medicines, when they arrived on the market, were so phenomenally expensive that they were out of reach of most homosexual men. In Japan, I heard a talk by a man who introduced the idea of a conspiracy theory to us, and that same year (2003), the maverick movie director Riyad Wadia, with whom I collaborated on the making of the cult short film *BomGay*, died because he refused to take his medicines.

COALITION POLITICS

Deviant sexuality marginalises those in possession of it as much as other identity-markers such as caste, class, race and gender. Yet for the mainstream, which has, over time, grudgingly accepted the politicisation of caste, class, race and gender in the fight for equality, sexuality (or sexual orientation) still remains something that embarrasses them.

The reasons for this are obvious: unlike the other four categories, which are a part of a person's public persona, sex is a private matter confined to the bedroom. To drag it into the public arena and discuss it openly requires us to compromise on our morals. Also, unlike the other four categories, one does not (have to) wear one's sexuality on one's sleeve. One can differentiate between a man and woman, or the upper and lower classes, or black and white people, on the basis of external appearance. The same can't be said about sexuality, because heterosexuality is assumed to be universal. How can we tell a gay man on the street?

While there may be some merit in these arguments, they certainly aren't reason enough for mainstream society to shy away from taking the bull by the horns. This, because victimhood and oppression are the same everywhere, regardless of what one's identity is. It is preposterous to suggest that a gay man's or gay woman's victimhood is any the less unjust than the victimhood of, say, a woman, a Dalit or a black. Yet, in a sense, that is exactly what we're saying.

In India, the issue of women's rights has been brought so much to the forefront that gender inequality is a subject that is hotly debated in the media, in academia and in politics. Though in reality women are still treated shabbily all over the country, patriarchal society has at least become aware of the need to grant women their fundamental rights. Legislation bolsters their case, because if a woman is harassed, no matter what the nature of the harassment is, the perpetrators can be sent to jail. Rape laws, as we know, have been recently amended to the advantage of women, and this has led to the incarceration of men across the social spectrum, from riff-raff on the one hand to celebrities on the other. In India, we have other women-centric laws like the anti-dowry law and the ultrasound law, under which people who could earlier get away with murder (literally) are now arrested.

Like women, the Dalits too have more or less won the battle for equality. They had their first messiah in Dr. B.R. Ambedkar, and later in poets like the late Namdeo Dhasal. Ever since Dhasal started his activist group, the Dalit Panthers, in the 1970s (inspired by the Black Panther movement in America), the Dalits have been militant in their war against caste-based oppression. Dr. Ambedkar was the principal architect of the Constitution of India, and his idealism led to the reservation policy that earmarks respectable government jobs for the Dalits, who spent their lives doing degrading, menial work like scavenging. In America, they call this "affirmative action". The Dalits also have laws that protect them against atrocities. If a Dalit claims he has been victimised in any way, the person he accuses can be arrested.

Contrast all this with the plight of homosexuals in India. We, too, have had our messiahs. Ashok Row Kavi of the Humsafar Trust, Bombay, was the first of them, and today several others, like our very own Bindumadhav Khire of the Samapathik Trust, Pune, have followed in his footsteps. But has anything changed? Section 377 of the Indian Penal Code, Macaulay's infamous anti-gay law of 1869, is still in place. Rather than protect a gay man from attack, this archaic and draconian law guarantees that the state too will join hands with a regressive society to skin the gay man alive. Unlike women and the Dalits, the gay community does not have a law that will scare away their oppressors from tormenting them. On the contrary, the existing laws give the oppressors a free hand to do what they will to their victim, and this can range from blackmail to extortion to rape to murder. And having indulged in criminal behaviour of the most obnoxious sort, the culprits can go scot-free, because, at the end of the day, they did what they did only to safeguard the morals of society.

How warped such thinking is!

PINK TRIANGLE

Last week, I visited the concentration camp at Dachau, Germany. Set up in 1932 by the Third Reich on the grounds of an ammunition factory near Munich, this was Nazi Germany's first concentration camp and served as the model for all its other concentration camps. The concentration camp was run by the *Schutzstaffel* (or Protection Battalion) that was better known by its initials, SS. (Perhaps it's no coincidence that one of our own political parties, whose politics, according to some, are similar to those of the *Schutzstaffel*, bear the same initials.)

One has to be brave to visit Dachau, for one sees here with one's own eyes all that we have merely read about in history books: the wooden barracks, designed for 5,000 prisoners, but which by 1942 were cramped with more than 12,000 prisoners huddled together; the gas chambers, euphemistically referred to as the "showers", where prisoners were suffocated to death with poisonous gases; the incinerators in which corpses were burned, some only half-dead. There are also archival photographs of the heaps of dead bodies that were left to rot in the open, for their number was so large that it was impossible to bury or cremate them.

Survivors speak of the shockingly inhuman treatment meted out to them in the camps: they had to do hard manual (and menial) labour from morning to evening; they were starved; they constantly received debilitating blows and kicks from the SS men and the Gestapo for even the smallest of lapses. The prisoners were kept so hungry that there are reports of some of them gnawing at the corpses of their comrades, like cannibals. Then there were diseases like typhoid that broke out in Dachau's unhygienic conditions and killed hundreds of inmates. The concentration camp at Dachau was surrounded by an outer wall enmeshed in barbed wire charged with electricity. A breakout attempt was thus bound to be fatal. However, some prisoners purposely tried to escape from the camp so that they could be shot dead by the SS, and thus be relieved of their suffering.

The largest group of prisoners in the concentration camps consisted of Jews whom Hitler wanted to exterminate. But a large number of the internees were homosexual men. The Nazis regarded homosexuals as "degenerate" and "foreign to the community". In 1935, Section 175 of the Criminal Code which made homosexuality a crime was applied to the prisoners at Dachau. Homosexual men were identified by a pink triangular patch that they were made to wear around their necks. The *SS* took it upon itself to torture and humiliate prisoners who wore the pink triangle. Their number steadily rose, from 170 in 1939, to over 600 by the end of the war in 1945. Like the Jews, the homosexuals belonged to assorted European nationalities, but the majority of them were Germans, French, Russians and Poles.

One of the homosexuals interned at Dachau was a Jewish wine dealer by the name of Leopold Obermayer. He was told he would be in the concentration camp for nine months, but this was eyewash. In truth, he was never released, and in 1942 he was sent from Dachau to another concentration camp at Mauthausen for "extermination through work". He died there on February 22nd, 1943.

Another homosexual prisoner at Dachau testifies to the slaps and kicks he got everyday from the *SS*. "How come you are here?" they asked him, and voyeuristically made him describe all his "offences". A fellow prisoner wrote:

> They wanted to know exactly what he had done, and how, and then they went after him all over again, slapping and kicking him. You could read the delight and sadism in their faces.

The Stonewall Riot of Greenwich Village, New York City, that symbolised gay revolution (and with which I began my column a few months ago), took place exactly 24 years after the concentration camps at Dachau and elsewhere were destroyed. Ironically, the Pink Triangle, which was once a hateful symbol of homosexual persecution, became its dazzling emblem. Today, to sport the pink triangle is not to remind oneself of the shameful excesses of the Nazis in the 1940s, but to announce one's (homo)sexuality to the world in a spirit of defiance and pride.

Pink triangles are available in gay merchandise shops all over the Western world in the form of T-shirts, rings and necklaces. I still possess the T-shirt I picked up in America in 1996, with a large pink triangle and the word "Visible" printed on it.

PARAGRAPH 175

Paragraph 175 (Section 175 in English) of the German Criminal Code made male homosexuality a crime. It was in force from 1871 to 1994. In 1935, the Nazis rigidified interpretations of Para 175, applying it not just to anal intercourse, but also to acts not involving physical contact, such as masturbating side by side, as gay men often did in washrooms. After that, convictions increased tenfold to about 8,000 per year. The Gestapo sent as many as 15,000 homosexual men to its concentration camps for "extermination through work". Most of them died there as a result of the torture and the exhaustion.

In February 1933, the Nazi Party launched its "purge" of "homophiles" (which was the term used to describe gay, lesbian and bisexual people). Gay groups were banned, books on homosexuality were burned, and homosexual men within the Nazi Party itself were killed. Kurt Hiller of the Magnus Hirschfeld Institute of Sex Research was arrested and sent to a concentration camp. The Gestapo constituted a special division to compile lists of homophiles that were forced to sexually conform to the "German [heterosexual] norm". Those who were lucky managed to flee Germany. Those who could not escape became Hitler's holocaust victims, along with the Jews.

The Nazis were against gay men because they saw them as "subversives" who got in the way of their (the Nazis') creation of a "master race". Heinrich Himmler, the leader of the *Schutzstaffel* (*SS*), glorified the masculine ideal (masculinity, in today's parlance) and the idea of a brotherhood among men. Homosexuality, according to him, contradicted these ideals. Himmler was alarmed that Germany had lost as many as four million men during the First World War, thus "upsetting the balance of the sexes in Germany". The need of the hour was for men to marry women and beget children, failing which the country was surely headed "for insignificance in fifty to one hundred years, [and] for burial in two hundred and fifty years." Homosexuals were to be despised, for they were "no longer capable of having sex with a female." While sending homosexuals to concentration camps, leniency was shown towards those who displayed "Aryan-ness" (that is, coming from true Germanic stock), and those who had managed to father children.

In the 12 years of Nazi rule between 1933 and 1945, as many as one lakh homosexual men were arrested by the Gestapo and the *SS*. Most of them were sent to regular prisons, but, as stated above, about 15,000 of them were sent to concentration camps. Statistics show that the death rate of homosexual prisoners in the concentration camps was considerably higher than that of other prisoners—whilst about 60% of the homosexual prisoners died here, the figure for other prisoners has been placed at roughly 40%. This is because homosexual men were treated in an unusually cruel manner by their captors. They were persecuted, not only by the German soldiers, but also by other prisoners, whom the soldiers encouraged. The persecution, needless to say, included sexual assault, highly plausible in the cramped concentration camps, in which, by 1945, the men were virtually sleeping on the wooden bunks one on top of the other.

The *SS*—and other, non-Jewish, prisoners—made sure that the gay men in the camps were given more arduous and life-threatening work than the others, and in the end, many of them were beaten to death. Those who did not die were used as guinea pigs by Nazi physicians to locate "a gay gene to cure any future Aryan children who were gay". But the most bone-chilling form of torture occurred when the SS men used homosexuals for target practice, aiming their guns and rifles at the downward-pointing pink triangles that the latter were forced to wear around their necks.

After the War, East Germany reverted to the old version of the law, restricting the definition of homosexuality to anal intercourse. In 1968, homosexuality was made a punishable offence only if it involved a boy under the age of eighteen. In 1988, East Germany abolished the law altogether. West Germany, on the other hand, retained the Nazi law till 1973, and revoked it altogether only in 1994, after the German reunification of 1989.

In 2002, the German government apologised to the gay community for its excesses during the Holocaust. A memorial "to the gay and lesbian victims of National Socialism" stands in the city of Cologne today. It reads, in German: *Totgeschlagen—Totgeschwiegen* ("Struck Dead—Hushed Up").

SHAME CULTURE

Queer scholars in India have called India's Hindu culture a "shame culture". They have contrasted this with what they call the "guilt culture" of the (Christian) West. According to them, what this means is that in India, with its emphasis on family relations, homosexuality, if made public, shames not just the homosexual himself, but the entire extended family of parents, children, siblings and relatives. Thus, homosexuality is frowned upon only if a person chooses to come out of the closet and live a gay lifestyle, which implies, among other things, that he does not get married. But if he performs his duty by getting married and starting a family, Hindu society has no qualms about his being a homosexual on the side.

It is for this reason that, in my view, *real* homophobia does not exist in India. What exists is a cosmetic homophobia that can easily be dealt with by tactfulness and cunning when it pertains to society in general, and by bribery when it pertains to *goondas* (thugs) and the police. Homophobia vanishes in the face of these things.

This view is also in keeping with the cultural fact that in India, and indeed in several parts of the East, one does not necessarily have to possess *one* sexuality, to the complete exclusion of the other. In other words, one can fluidly be both homosexual and heterosexual at the same time. What aids this, of course, is heterosexism, which serves as its alibi. So a man, no matter how feminine he may be in his behaviour and mannerisms, is assumed to be sexually attracted to women. Conversely, a woman, no matter how masculine she may be in her behaviour and mannerisms, is assumed to be sexually attracted to men. When such beliefs permeate our thinking, there is no room for homophobia, the precondition for which is the straitjacketing of all human beings as *either* homosexual *or* heterosexual.

Urban India has gone a step further. It has allowed its homosexual children to live homosexual lives provided they follow all the cardinal principles of heteronormativity: they should find partners who are of the same age and social class (and perhaps caste) as themselves, and they should be monogamous. If these conditions are fulfilled, homosexuality no longer shames the family.

It's different in the Christian West, where homosexuality, traditionally, has been seen as a sin against the will of God. This naturally breeds *real* homophobia in the minds of the orthodox and the devout. It is a homophobia that cannot be dealt with by worldly tools like tactfulness and bribery, for it involves God. The Vatican's homophobia goes to such an extent that it once said that the world had to be saved from homosexuality, just as its rain forests had to be saved: failure to save the world from either the one or the other would lead to its destruction.

A sin is supposed to be atoned for or expiated, without which the sinner remains guilty for the rest of his life, and is cast into hell upon death: that is what queer scholars mean by calling the culture of the West a guilt culture. A homosexual sin can only be atoned for if the homosexual person concerned becomes a heterosexual, not by feigning or faking it, as we do in India's shame culture, but by getting it genuinely "cured". There are pious Christians who, even in the 21st century, believe that homosexuality can be cured by prayer and clean thoughts.

Such apostles of God are shocked by the fact that the West has gotten so "degenerate" today, that it upholds homosexuality in even its most perverse forms. Hence the rain forests simile. One of the things that irks this lobby the most is gay marriage: to their mind, gay marriage destroys the very sanctity of the hallowed institution, which belongs exclusively to heterosexuals. For marriage is merely a means to an end (the end being the birth of children), but homosexuals have made marriage an end in itself. Homosexuals are thus seen as agents of the Devil, fit to be annihilated.

To me, this is what true homophobia means. The homophobia of the Nazi *SS* was *real* punitive homophobia that sent homosexuals to concentration camps. The homophobia of our *SS* is cosmetic extortionist homophobia that can be dealt with by a simple thing like an ATM card.

You, Me and "Hum"

Manju Ramanan

Manju Ramanan, brought up in Baroda but based in Dubai, is a journalist and writer.

My title was inspired by the Hindi film *U, Me aur Hum* (dir. Ajay Devgn 2008), which means "you, me and us", but the inspiration ends there. The film is about love in the shadow of Alzheimer's, while I wish to show how "the Other"—"you", referring here to Indian tribals and denotified tribal communities—entered my life ("me"), blasting away deep-rooted prejudices and helping me gain a new perspective on the world ("*hum*", or "us").

I was born into an educated Tamil Brahmin family in Gujarat, and my introduction to "the Other" started with prejudices. I was around eight or ten years old, growing up in Baroda in the '80s, when I noticed how some of the plumbers or masons from the Waghri community who came to our home to repair a toilet or fix a broken wall or tile would refuse to take the glass of water that I offered them. They would insist that I pour it from the glass into their cupped palm and then they would drink it.

I was excited about the drama surrounding this event, but ignorant of the long tradition of prejudice of which it was part. My grandmother explained to me that since they were tribals (she would refer to them as Scheduled Castes) and worked among the toilets, *etc.*, they were presumably unclean and so they wouldn't want to leave any germs on the glass we offered. But didn't the germs affect *them*, too, since they drank the same water, and that too with their bare hands?

Some questions were left unanswered, and this was my sketchy initial introduction to "the Other". To the best of my childhood understanding and imagination, they were people who were unlike us: they lived far away in deep forests, a long way from technology and advancement, they ate differently, and their women smoked *beedis* (rolled tobacco leaves). I was also told that the tribal gods were not as benign-looking as ours. The story that fascinated me most as a child was one about the "Treemen of Travancore"—about tribals who lived in the trees. My father encountered it as a chapter in a school textbook in the '40s and recollected that it was written by a European traveller who had met and lived with this tribe—who lived up in the trees and feasted on tadpoles! (For the "Treemen", see Iyer 1941.)

Other prejudices were derived from Hindi cinema, which reinforced the idea that tribals (or *adivasis*) came mostly from the forest and usually wore grass skirts, clothes made of bark, or other revealing costumes. They sang and danced differently to the heroes and heroines of the films, and their songs were incomprehensible but catchy ("Hum Bewafa Hargiz Na The" in *Shalimar*, 1978, released in the USA as *Raiders of Shalimar*, is a good example of such a song). Lee Fawk's *Phantom* comics, depicting white men ruling the tribal world of Africa, reinforced such ideas.

My prejudice would have carried on blissfully uninterrupted if things had not changed in college at Baroda. I was enjoying some inspirational English literature teaching at the Maharaja Sayajirao University, and learning about literary theory and the politicisation of language, while doing postgraduate work. A highly respected professor, Dr. Ganesh Devy, a Sahitya Akademi winner and well-reputed scholar, quit his university job to start the Bhasha Research and Publication Center (BRPC), which set out to document tribal languages that were on the verge of extinction. The BRPC successfully launched a tribal magazine, *Dhol*, which documented tribal languages. In due course, it initiated a historical movement to address a pertinent part of tribal life—human rights. In 1998, the BRPC organised the Verrier Elwin lecture series in Baroda, commemorating the celebrated tribal activist Verrier Elwin (1902-64), a Christian missionary who had given up his vocation in order to work with Mahatma Gandhi, and found his calling with the Baiga and Gond tribes of Central India. Elwin married a tribal woman, and served as Deputy Director of the Anthropological Survey of India upon its formation in 1945 (Guha 1999).

The first Verrier Elwin lecture was delivered by Magsaysay award winner and tribal activist Mahasweta Devi. She spoke about Budhan Sabar, a denotified tribal (DNT) killed in police custody. Budhan belonged to the Sabar tribe from Purulia district in West Bengal. He was travelling with his wife Shyamali Sabar to attend a wedding in a nearby village when the police inspector from Burabazar Police Station arrested him. The next day, his dead body was handed over to his wife—and the postmortem report stated that he had committed suicide in police custody.

It was bizarre, since Budhan had no reasons for suicide and was about to attend a joyous occasion. The Sabars who worked closely with Mahasweta Devi told her about Budhan's death and, following her advice, did not cremate the body. To reassure the police that the body had been burned, however, the Sabars cleverly cremated an effigy, while Shyamali dug a hole in her hut, buried her husband's body in it, covered it with a mat and sat on it in mourning, until the moment when Mahasweta Devi arrived with a lawyer and another doctor. The second autopsy that was then conducted proved that his death had occurred *before* he was allegedly found hanging. Other evidence too pointed towards his death having been murder rather than suicide (Devi 1999).

Mahasweta Devi's speech moved me deeply. This, in combination with the emotions that I was experiencing in literature class, where there was a lot of heightened classroom discussion on literary theory connected with the politicisation of language but hardly any follow-up in the form of action, compelled me to volunteer for the BRPC, which had now started the Denotified Tribals Rights Action Group (DNT RAG) to work for justice in the matter of Budhan's custodial death.

For my postgraduate degree, I had chosen to study institutional racism—a term coined by Stokely Carmichael of the Black Panther Party, who, in the late '60s, defined it as "the collective failure of an organisation to provide an appropriate and professional service to people because of their colour, culture, or ethnic origin"—and what it had done to three minority communities of Canada: the First Nations, the Japanese- and the Chinese-Canadians. In class, I was learning how prejudiced and subversive laws and regulations formulated by imperialism influenced and shaped the writings of the above-mentioned minorities in Canada. Imperial rule had annihilated so many tribes there by hunting them like animals, gifting them diseased blankets and wiping them all out, or "befriending them" for trade. In the book *Shananditti: The Last of the Beothuks*, the last living member of the Beothuk tribe from Newfoundland tells her story (Winter 1975). At the BRPC, I had the chance to meet DNTs, some of whom had been born in police custody, had endured third-degree torture in jails, or were victims of false accusation due to an outdated and prejudiced system.

According to Devy (1998), the estimated population of the DNTs is around 60 million, and in India there are about 191 communities that were once wrongly "notified" as "criminal tribes", owing to the colonial government's lack of understanding of the nomadic way of life. They were restricted by law to specific localities, prevented from moving, put to unpaid labour and stigmatised beyond redemption. After their "denotification" in 1952, these communities, now known as DNTs, continued to suffer stigma, social isolation and acute economic disadvantage. Utterly dispossessed, these landless, illiterate and hounded people have been unsuccessfully trying to shake off their identity.

It was appalling to learn how prejudice became a potent weapon of domination and discrimination. According to the historian and tribal activist Ajay Dandekar, in his essay "The Hegemony of Silence":

> In the 19th century, the colonial government decided to categorise these pastoral nomads, itinerant traders and other disbanded groups who include the members of defeated native armies and other wandering communities as different from those settled agriculturists of a fixed abode. The then administration decided that these wandering communities could not be situated within preconceived categorisations—whether administrative, economic or social. This was the context to the passage of the "Criminal Tribes Act of 1871" or Act XXVII (henceforth referred to as the CTA) (16).

Dandekar explains how it is important to look at the legal provisions of the CTA. The act stated:

> Whereas it is expedient to provide for the registration, surveillance and control of certain criminal tribes and eunuchs, it is thereby enacted as follows: This Act may be called "The Criminal Tribes Act, 1871".

> [Commencement, repealed by Act XVI of 1874, Section 1 and Schedule, Part I.] This section and section 20 extend to the whole of British India [...] to be in force in the whole or any part of the territories under its government (17).

The CTA gave unrestricted access to the imperial government to prey on the communities listed under it. As Devy (1998) says:

> Many of the wandering minstrels, fakirs, petty traders, rustic transporters and disbanded groups of soldiers were included by the British in their list of criminal groups. During the first half of the 19th century, the tribes in the North West frontier had been declared "criminal tribes". This category became increasingly open ended and by 1871, the British had prepared an official list of Criminal Tribes. An act to regulate criminal tribes was passed that year. For instance, Bhils who had fought the British rule in Kandesh and on the banks of Narmada and were convicted under section 110 of the IPC were to be recognised as criminal tribes.

This act was modified in 1952, five years after Indian Independence, but it was merely a name change. The "Criminal Tribes" were re-christened "Denotified Tribes"—the criminality being removed solely from the nomenclature—though in reality attitudes towards the DNTs and discrimination meted out to them stayed the same. What is more, this was followed by the introduction of a series of acts generally known as Habitual Offenders Acts!

> The HOAs preserved most of the provisions of the former CT Acts, except the premise implicit in it that an entire community can be "born" criminal. Apparently, the denotification and the passing of the HOAs should have ended the misery of the communities penalised under the CT Act. But that has not happened. The police force as well as the people in general were taught to look upon the "Criminal Tribes" as born criminals during the colonial times. That attitude continues to persist even today (Devy 1998).

Sidelined by mainstream society, without too many opportunities owing to the prejudice associated with their names, castes, caste certificates and surnames, many DNTs are naturally pulled into the world of petty crime—ironically reinforcing the very prejudice against them.

On my first day at the BRPC, I met a Gond tribal man from the city who had come to meet Dr. Devy. I was horrified to see that he had a dagger stuck to his left wrist, which was bleeding profusely. To arrest the blood flow, he had used a dirty kerchief. It was a perfect anti-climax when, having read my thoughts, he let me into his secret: "*Ben, yeh to spring hai*" ("Sister, this is a spring"), showing me how the dagger was a roughly-made gadget, the blood animal blood, and the whole thing merely a ploy to garner sympathy and collect money from passers-by. This, I learned later, was one of the professions chosen by DNTs, involving a macabre kind of entertainment from the show of self-mutilation.

A case that happened at about the same time was that of a tribal from the Bajania community who had been killed by the upper caste Patels for stealing a bottle gourd from their orchard. Ironically, he belonged to a group of worshipers of Goddess Bahucharaji—a group that refrains from eating gourd as part of their religious rules. The dying man had named his killers, but power and bribes had prevented justice from being done. Another case was that of Pinya Hari Kale, who was arrested and then killed in police custody, though his death was investigated and compensation awarded (D'Souza 1999).

The campaign by the DNT RAG took up issues like these and received an overwhelming response from the denotified communities—soon a journal called *Budhan* was started, the Budhan Sabar case was re-opened and it was proved that he was killed in police custody and did not commit suicide. His wife Shyamali Sabar was awarded compensation, something never before heard of.

As Susan Abraham in her article 'Steal or I'll Call You a Thief' (1999) has written:

> In a public interest litigation filed by Mahasweta Devi before the Calcutta High Court after the death of Budhan Sabar in police custody, Justice Ruma Pal passed a historical judgement on August 6th, 1998, ordering a CBI enquiry into Budhan Sabar's death, the immediate transfer of inspector Ashoke Roy and Rs. 1 lakh [100,000 rupees, approx. 2,200 USD in 2010—*Ed.*] compensation to Budhan Sabar's widow. In

> the case of Pinya Hari Kale, a writ petition has been filed by Laxman Gaikwad in the Bombay High Court (1753).

This stirred up a hornet's nest, and cases of atrocities against DNTs and custodial deaths started pouring in from different states of India. We received photographs, documents, complaints and cases on a regular basis, many of which became stories for the journal *Budhan*. The stand that the DNT RAG took was challenging—through networking with academics, activists, writers and tribal leaders and the media across India, it had to create awareness of the issue—an issue that involved half a million people and deep-rooted prejudices, left over from the colonial era, that DNTs are genetically criminal.

The colonial administration in the 19th century helped propagate this idea of criminality by coming up with a list of criminal tribes across India, sometimes cordoning off areas they lived in, making it mandatory for them to report to the nearby police station every day and, most brutal of all, introducing the CT list into the curriculum for police schools across India (D'Souza), so that both British as well as Indian students would learn to hate and condemn the CTs. On the other hand, there was the challenge of not over-romanticising the DNT population—after all, some of them *did* indulge in petty crime and thievery (see Dutt 2003). The DNT RAG worked towards winning justice for vulnerable DNTs who were victims of a flawed system. As Devy (2008) says:

> We had exposed a long-festering wound. As a leader of that campaign, I had to give very serious thought to turning the anger and frustration among the demonised, brutalised and politically vandalised DNT into a constructive energy. I decided to use the most ancient method of getting people angry without making them destructive—theatre. My experience with handling the violence within the minds of these communities has left me convinced that theatre is probably the most powerful cultural means of sensitising communities on the mutual entanglement and dependence of economic, social and cultural rights of several competing and clashing social sectors.

Using theatre as a means of working with the DNTs can be well illustrated with the DNT RAG's work with the Chharas, an educated community of

DNTs from the Kubernagar area near Ahmedabad in Gujarat. The Chharas are known to brew liquor illegally with help from none other than the state police—ironically, in a state where alcohol is prohibited! Police personnel pay an inter-departmental bribe to be stationed at Chharanagar to be able to extort money from the Chharas for indulging in a state-prohibited activity (Ramanan 2006).

The DNT RAG started work with the Chharas by setting up a library on their premises, and getting together a group of Chharas to form their own theatre group, aptly named the Budhan Theatre Group. Headed by Daxin Chhara, the group stages plays based on true incidents of atrocities against denotified Indian tribals who are treated as born criminals by the legal system and as thieves by mainstream society, including plays about the treatment of Budhan Sabar of Purulia, West Bengal, Deepak Pawar of Maharashtra, and so on. The plays reflect the inhuman treatment meted out to DNTs and appeal to people to respect them and take their human dignity into account. As Daxin told me:

> Budhan Theatre is a volunteer theatre group of [the] Chhara tribe. [The] Chhara tribe is one of the denotified tribes, [...] branded by law as "born criminals" by [the] British. Presently, based in Ahmedabad, this community is a "forever suspect" in the eye[s] of law and order and mainstream society and treated as a "hardcore criminal". Police atrocity and harassment is a regular practice among the Chhara tribe as well as among other denotified tribes of India. Budhan Theatre is trying to remove the criminal stigma attached to the Chhara tribe through theatre, which we believe is our inherited talent. Through theatre, we are sensitising society towards social acceptance and legal justice. The DNTs have lost their identity due to living on the fringes of society. So many years after Independence, these communities and their people [still] have no constitutional guarantees. Budhan Theatre is a cultural platform to protest and to raise the voice of the denotified and nomadic communities and fight for social justice and human dignity (E-mail from Daxin Chhara; see also *Budhan Theatre*, website).

The Bhasha Trust established the Adivasi Academy at Tejgadh in 1999. Since 2000, it has been teaching young men and women Tribal

Studies—the study and understanding of how *adivasis* perceive the world. The idea is to make students reflect on their own situation, to motivate them and help them start about the great task of empowering *adivasi* villages by helping them to become self-reliant. The academy offers short-term training in microfinance, and diploma courses in Tribal Rights, Food Security and Development, Publication and Rural Journalism, and Tribal Arts and Museum Studies.

The varied activities of the BRPC shaped my perspective on the world. In December 1998, the DNT RAG organised the All India DNT Convention, at which various DNTs from all over India along with theorists like Gayatri Chakravorty Spivak and historians like Romila Thapar participated in a common forum. Probably for the first time in their lives, many DNTs realised that people like themselves existed all over India—and shared a common heritage of prejudice.

All of us watched wide-eyed as we discovered the wealth that Indian tribal communities possessed—the history and culture that they had inherited—as well as the subversive laws that they were battling, years after India won Independence. This included, for example, a tribe from Maharashtra who were adept at sign language—and who demonstrated their unique skill. A man standing at one end of a room with a big *dhol* (drum) asked me my name and, after I had whispered it to him, he beat a tune accompanied by some hand movements and his tribesman standing at the other end of the room shouted it out. It is said that the tribe used their unique ability as a means of passing on information about enemy attacks during the rule of the famous Maratha king, Chhatrapati Shivaji.

One of the most remarkable tribal men that I met was the former pickpocket, now turned award-winning writer, Laxman Gaikwad, from the Pardhi tribe. During an interview (I had become a journalist with *The Times of India* in Baroda), he explained how things had changed for him after he "abandoned the blade and took to the pen". His 1987 autobiography, *Uchalya* (The Branded), was honoured by Sahitya Akademi, India's National Academy of Letters in 1988.

> The razor blade was our Laxmi. We would pray to the God of Instruments (Ayudha) before every outing. We would cut a chicken with the same blade and spray its blood on the participants, and we prayed:

> "God, we pray for success in today's thieving mission. Rescue us from the police if we get caught..." (based on Vikas Kamat's translation of excerpts from the original Marathi, online).

As for fear of the police, who usually hunted them down, he says:

> We were very afraid of the police. I cannot count the times I have defecated in my clothes during police tortures. My community members started hating my grandfather, as he was giving inside information to the police. "Because of Lingappa [his grandfather] life has become hard; we are not able to feed our wives and children," they complained. One day, they held a meeting to decide the next course of action. That night, they stuffed grandpa's mouth with rags, and killed him with an axe. They even burnt his body to destroy any evidence. That is how grandmother became head of the family (based on Kamat's translation).

This subaltern world existed parallel to my own—had been shielded from me, presumably by my protected upbringing, a life that had the time and the luxury to ponder over and romanticise suffering, though without feeling even a pinch of the harsh reality. But for "them", it was the only way of life that they knew.

This was brought home to me when I interviewed several members of the DNT community, including Sushma Andhare from the Kolhati community. Sushma had resisted family pressure, and endured neglect and isolation, because she wanted to study, rather than join the family profession of being a *tamasha* dancer, where young girls are taught the traditional *tamasha* dance and soon exposed to the ugly world of prostitution. Mentored by the DNT activist, Laxman Mane, Sushma opted to study and do a doctorate instead, and now has several books to her credit.

Colonial attitudes towards aboriginal peoples are common throughout the world—and long after the end of colonialism—and upper caste attitudes towards the *adivasis* of India are an example of this. While one can blame imperialism and the various tools it used to contain what it believed to be criminal, the casteist mindset hasn't allowed this prejudice to be exorcised in the way that it should have been.

Movements like the DNT RAG have now moved online, through *Mukt-Saad*, a web publication from Baroda maintained by India's National Folklore Support Centre, which is contributing to the gradual sensitisation in India to the issue of DNTs.

The DNTs are part of my life—they have shaped the course my life has taken. They are instrumental in helping me in my quest to blur the difference between "you", "me" and "*hum*".

Three Poems

Meena Kandasamy

Meena Kandasamy is a well-known poet, novelist, actress, translator, feminist and social activist; she also has a doctorate in sociolinguistics.

ONE-EYED

the pot sees just another noisy child
the glass sees an eager and clumsy hand
the water sees a parched throat slaking thirst
but the teacher sees a girl breaking the rule
the doctor sees a medical emergency
the school sees a potential embarrassment
the press sees a headline and a photofeature

dhanam sees a world torn in half.
her left eye, lid open but light slapped away,
the price for a taste of that touchable water.

REVERENCE::NUISANCE

On walls of reception counters
and staircases of offices, hospitals, firms
and other "secular" institutions—
pictures of Hindu Gods are painted.

so that casual people walking in (or up or down)
fear to spit on the adorned walls.

But still looking around or climbing:
you can always find the work done
a irregular red border underlining the walls
owing so much to betel juice and spit.

And on cheap roadside compound walls
that don't bear "Stick No Bills" messages or
cinema and political posters—the Gods once again
are advertised. And captioned with legends that read
"Do not Urinate". And yet, the Gods are covered with
layers of smelly urine—they don't retaliate.

Tolerance is a very holy concept.
Or like someone said,
the Caste Gods deserve
the treatment they get.

MULLIGATAWNY DREAMS

anaconda. candy. cash. catamaran.
cheroot. coolie. corundum. curry.
ginger. mango. mulligatawny.
patchouli. poppadom. rice.
tatty. teak. vetiver.

i dream of an english
full of the words of my language.

an english in small letters
an english that shall tire a white man's tongue
an english where small children practise with smooth
round pebbles in their mouth to spell the right zha
an english where a pregnant woman is simply stomach-child-lady
an english where the magic of black eyes and brown bodies replaces the glamour of eyes in dishwater blue shades and the airbrush romance of pink white cherry blossom skins
an english where love means only the strange frenzy
between a man and his beloved, not between him and his car
an english without the privacy of its many rooms
an english with suffixes for respect
an english with more than thirty six words to call the sea
an english that doesn't belittle brown or black men and women
an english of tasting with five fingers
an english of talking love with eyes alone

and i dream of an english

where men
of that spiky, crunchy tongue
buy flower-garlands of jasmine
to take home to their coy wives
for the silent demand of a night of wordless whispered love . . .

Cultural Diversity in the North East of India

Dibyajyoti Sarma

Dibyajyoti Sarma is a poet, an editor and an academic. By day, he is a PhD scholar, who has published papers on Indian Writing in English and on Queer Theory. In the evening, he is the senior copy editor with an Indian national daily. And at night, he is a creative writer, who has published short stories and two volumes of poetry, Glimpses of a Personal History *(2004) and* Pages from an Unfinished Autobiography *(2014).*

He was born in Assam.

According to reports, there are at least 40 different terrorist outfits (all working from somewhere between India and Myanmar), from the seven states of North East India (Assam, Meghalaya, Manipur, Tripura, Mizoram, Nagaland and Arunachal Pradesh). All of them have similar goals; they want geographical independence or political self-rule for the ethnic communities they represent. In an increasingly fragmented world, where Hindus are fighting for their supremacy and Muslims are fighting for theirs, the fight for the rights of an ethnic community sounds valid. The question, however, is whether these demands are feasible.

There are at least 100 different communities in these seven North Eastern states, with their own languages and cultures, with their own gods and their own wines and their own clothes. Yet, for centuries, they have lived together, sharing the same geography. Politically, it may not have been an easy coexistence, yet it was achieved. Let us consider this diversity, how it flourished, and why, now, the communities are clamouring for political isolation.

WHOSE LAND IS IT ANYWAY?

A few months back, there was uproar when the ruling Congress Party in the state Legislative Assembly of Assam, in the North East of India, could not answer a simple question concerning the national identity of the state. The question was: "Who are the Assamese people?"

On the face of it, it was a simple question, which warranted a simple answer: "The Assamese people are the people who reside in Assam."

However, in the context of the volatile socio-political reality of the state since the country's Independence in 1947, the question becomes a veritable minefield. Before answering it, the Party needed to answer another question: "Does permanent residence makes you a part of the state?"

And this leads to a further question: "How long must a community live in a politically defined geographical area in order to claim to be a part of the national identity?"

These questions point the finger at the issue of the illegal Bangladeshi migrants in Assam, which has been a subject of emotional political debate for the last 50 years without any sign that the issue will ever be resolved.

DEFINING ASSAM WITHIN THE NORTH EAST OF INDIA

Before we can discuss the Bangladeshi, largely Muslim, migrants, and how and why they are a threat to the very fabric of cultural diversity of the state and the region, we must first understand the political history of Assam.

Assam is a land-locked geographical entity, set amidst hills and valleys, rivers and bogs, and surrounded by six other Indian states, Arunachal Pradesh, Manipur, Mizoram, Meghalaya, Tripura and Nagaland, all of which at one point of history or another were part of the "Greater Assam". In this context, Assam was the centre of the mainstream culture, a port of call, so to speak, to disseminate knowledge of the modern world among the ethnic communities cocooned in the hills and the valleys. The state also shares international borders with Bangladesh, Myanmar and Bhutan.

While the vast majority of the population of Assam, in both the Brahmaputra and Barak River valleys, became assimilated into mainstream Indian culture, the ethnic communities in Assam and elsewhere in the six other states have remained insular.

Assam received the mainstream Indian cultural influences through a series of epoch-making migrations, and its interaction with the outside cultures. For example, even before the arrival of the Ahoms, a tribal king of Kamatapur (the region between Assam and Bengal) had invited 12 households of Brahmins and 12 households of Kayasthas from Gour in the Ganges Valley to spread Hinduism among the local masses.

The strength of Assamese cultural identity reached its zenith during the time of the Ahom King, Rudra Singha (1696–1714). By then, more than half of the North East was part of the Ahom Kingdom and the royal dynasty, an ethnic group that had migrated from either China or Burma, had all but shed its tribal heritage. They became Hindus, and took Hindu names, while a lot of their customs found their way into the mainstream "Hindu" culture. For example, most of the names of the rivers in Assam have tribal roots.

The final inspiration in this saga of cultural assimilation and diversity was the Indian struggle for freedom movement in the late 19th and early 20th century. Before that, there had been the Bengal Renaissance, when young Assamese men, forced to learn English in Calcutta, had turned inwards towards their own culture and sought a revival, through their own language and idioms. Nor should we underestimate the contribution of the American Baptist missionaries, especially Reverend Nathan Brown, who wrote the first Assamese dictionary and laid the foundation for modern Assamese language and literature with the establishment of the first Assamese magazine, *Arunodoi* (The Rising Sun) in 1846. Thus, as the fire of the struggle for freedom movement spread, mainstream Assam was at the forefront.

Unlike the cultural identity of the other Indian states, where ethnic communities were also part of the mainstream culture, the cultural assimilation in the North East was less rigid and more fluid. Madhab Kandali did the first translation of Valmiki's *Ramayana* into a local Indian language—into Old Assamese—long before Tulsidas's *Sri Ram Charit Manas*. At the same time, the national festival of Assam, Bihu, has a distinctly tribal origin.

This, however, could not bring together the numerous ethnic communities in Assam. There are several reasons for this. Most of these ethnic communities lived / live within a particular geographic territory, where communication with other communities is often difficult, owing to the rugged nature of the geography of the land (even today, there are tribes in the forests of Arunachal Pradesh that have scant contact with the outside world. The landscape is treacherous and there are no roads. The only possible communication is by helicopter, if the weather is good).

These small communities (and they are numerous) are defined by their own customs and rituals and their inherent pride in their community. From the beginning, they were at constant war with each other (especially in Nagaland) to maintain their ethnic pride. Before the arrival of the British, the mainstream rulers left these communities to their own devices. Of course, there were contacts, but these were mostly economic. For example, the Nocte tribe in the Tirap Valley of Arunachal Pradesh supplied salt from the hot springs to the Ahom kings, while the Nagas supplied timber, woollen garments and other products.

This interaction between different communities (each with its own language) gave rise to a lingua franca called Nagamese. It was a mixture of Assamese and local languages. Over the years, it has come to include a large number of Hindi and English words as well.

With regard to the insular communities on the fringes of the North East, it was the British colonial power and the missionaries who built the first important bridge. As Christianity replaced the animist religions of the tribes (the mainstream Hindu religion had not had any obvert problem with animism, since animism is also a part of the larger Hindu canon), it became a common thread to unite the different warring tribes. This shift, however, remained superficial, as the tribes continued to follow the old customs and rituals despite converting to Christianity.

The British did not help either. As part of their famous divide and rule policy, they discouraged cultural integration of different tribes. All they were interested in was profits.

There were kings, and there were colonisers, and now there is a democracy, which has redefined the traditional geographical boundaries. Earlier, each ethnic community had a village or a set of villages, the land beyond which—the forests and the hills—had belonged to no one. The communities would cultivate this land that belonged to no one and gather sustenance from the forest that belonged to no one. After Independence, these free natural resources became part of the state, a concept that the communities were not aware of, and a system which did not offer the communities a chance of participation.

TRACKING THE MIGRATION PATTERN

This leads us to the question: who does the land belong to?

According to the scriptures, in ancient times the region, known as Pragjyotishpur, was ruled by the Danava dynasty, a descendent of which, Bhagadutta, was said to have fought in the Mahabharata War. In the scriptures, the Danavas were a non-Aryan indigenous people. Anthropologically speaking, then, the Bodos were perhaps the first indigenous inhabitants of the land. Everyone else came later, and there are histories to verify the facts.

In short, Assam is a land of migrants learning to co-habit with the indigenous people. The Tai Ahoms, who ruled most of t Pavagadh Pavagadh he region for more than 600 years, came from China (or Burma). The Kochs came from Tibet (or Burma?). Meanwhile, there was a steady migration from mainland India, especially from Gour, which accounts for today's non-tribal Assamese population.

Before the arrival of the colonial power in Assam, the geographical reality was very different. Discounting ancient history, even if we start in medieval times, with the arrival of the Tai Ahoms from the Far East, in 1228, the region had numerous kingdoms, big and small, spilling over the boundary of today's North East.

For example, a large chunk of Bangladesh, especially the Sylhet district, was part of the erstwhile Kachari Kingdom, with its capital in Dimapur. The Ahoms ruled Upper Assam for nearly 600 years. The Kingdom of the Koch, a Tibeto-Burmese group, extended from western Assam to present-day North Bengal. The Sutiya Kingdom ruled all the regions on the north bank of the Brahmaputra while the Kacharis ruled Central and Southern Assam.

Besides these, there were numerous small "kingdoms", which paid tribute to the bigger dynasties. In fact, every tribe and sub-tribe in the region had its own system of polity. There were, of course, wars, for political and economic gains, but the winner never tried to impose its own culture on the subjugated. Diverse cultural practices were allowed free rein.

According to the "People of India" project, which studied 115 ethnic groups in Assam, 79 (69%) identify themselves regionally, 22 (19%) locally, and three trans-nationally. The earliest settlers were Austroasiatic, followed by Tibeto-Burman, Indo-Aryan, and Tai–Kadai speakers.

Forty-five languages are spoken by different communities, including three major language families: Austroasiatic (5), Sino-Tibetan (24) and Indo-European (12). Three of the spoken languages do not fall into any of these categories. There is a high degree of bilingualism.

There are 23 notified Scheduled Tribes (STs) in Assam with the Bodos (40.9%) making half of the total ST population (around 13%) of the state. The other STs (on the plains and in the hills) include the Mishing, Miri, Karbi, Rabha, Kachari, Lalung, Barman in Cachar, Borokachar, Deori, Hajai, Mech, Dimasa, Hajong, Singhphho, Khampti, Garo, Biate, Khasi, Jaintia, Synteng, Pnar, War, Bhoi, Lyngngam, Kuki, Chakma, and Hmar.

THE PROBLEMS OF NEW MIGRATIONS

There are two reasons why people migrated to Assam and continue to do so. There was land aplenty. There was a time, in the heartland of Assam, when people could just go and mark a boundary on a piece of land and call it their own. There was more land than there were people. And the land was remarkably fertile. It was said that in Assam if you threw a mango seed a tree would grow.

This is one of the reasons why the Mughal Army, which attacked Assam 18 times, never succeeded. The Mughals did not come to Assam to settle. They would have been allowed to do so. They came to claim land that was already occupied. They had come to destroy the local cultures, and so they were opposed.

The British, on the other hand, took over Assam, and the whole of the North East, in a sly manner. They were not interested in the land at all. They were interested in the wealth that the land could generate. They prospected for oil. They started the tea gardens. Still, there was enough land for everyone, so no-one complained. When the British could not find local labourers to work for them on the tea plantations, they imported people from Bihar and Odisha. Still no one complained, as there were jobs for everyone.

The British, however, successfully destroyed the fabric of traditional life in Assam, especially among the middle class, when they lured them away to education and jobs. This was the first break in the communal identity that existed in the pre-British era. Earlier, people from one community would spend all their lives in one place. This would be the beginning and the end of their world. After the arrival of the British, people started to travel around, started to see other people and find associations.

This became all the more apparent with the Independence movement. One small community could not fight the forces of Empire. But all the communities together could. Thus, the idea of a Greater Assam was born. Thus, the idea that this Greater Assam should be a part of mainland India under the leadership of Mahatma Gandhi came to be formulated.

India became independent and Assam became a state. It was not an easy transition, but it happened. The biggest casualty in this entire drama was the loss of identity of the communities. They were now part of a politically constructed, unreal identity of being "Assamese".

It did not matter much. People still had their land, their home and their source of livelihood, which also helped keep alive their inherent identity. Being Assamese did not rob them of anything. Hence, no one bothered about the continued migration of communities, from Nepal, Rajasthan, UP and Bihar, and from East Bengal, now part of Pakistan.

Things started to change with the Bangladesh War in 1972. Earlier, communities who came to settle in Assam had come in smaller groups, they were less visible, and they were easily absorbed. Now, migration started to take place on a large scale, first with government-sponsored refugees, and then, illegally. Still, the existing population did not have much to complain about. There was land for everybody. Most of these migrants from Bangladesh settled down in the low-lying areas and the river islands, places where others would not go.

Since then, two things have happened. First, the population has increased massively in the last 40 or so years. Secondly, this flow of migration has never stopped, unlike all the migrations of the past.

According to the 2011 census, the total population of Assam was 31,169,272. The total population of the state has thus increased from 26,638,407 to 31,169,272 in the last ten years, with a growth rate of 16.93%. Of the 27 districts of Assam, eight districts registered a rise in the decadal population growth rate. Religious minority-dominated districts like Dhubri, Goalpara, Barpeta, Morigaon, Nagaon, Hailakandi, and so on, have recorded growth rates ranging from 20% to 24% during the last decade. On the other hand, eastern Assam districts like Sivasagar, Jorhat, *etc.*, registered around 9% population growth. These districts do not have any international border. So we know that the excess rise in population has come from the Bangladeshi migrants.

With the rise in population, the availability of land is shrinking. This has given rise to a conflict between the communities who were settled here before and those who came later. Moreover, since the flow of migration has never stopped, these migrating communities have never severed their ties with their "homeland" and become assimilated, as happened with the migrating communities of the past. They could never create their own identities and be part of the Assamese identity; instead, they remained outsiders, which made them an easy target.

It is said that Assamese people are the most hospitable in the world. It is true. The Assamese people did not mind giving away their land as long as they had enough. Now, there is no longer enough land, and it has become a struggle for survival—between those who came first and those who came later. This is one way of explaining what happened in Kokrajhar District in 2012, where at least 77 people died and 400,000 people was displaced in the violence between indigenous Bodos and East Bengal Muslim migrants.

THE POLITICS OF RELIGION

That new migrants from Bangladesh taking over resources belonging to the indigenous people of the North East is just a part of the problem. The land is still generous, and the people are still innocent, and would have accommodated these new migrants if they had been willing to assimilate into the local culture. But this did not happen.

The new migrants continued to hold on to their own language, Bangla, and their religion, Islam. Whilst earlier a particular ethnic community would flourish within a defined geographical location, the new migrants settled down wherever there happened to be space. Whilst earlier, one community would interact with other communities for socio-political and economic reasons, now the new migrants started to communicate among themselves, even after settling in different parts of the region, with their religion becoming the centre of their identity.

This was facilitated by the political manoeuvre of divide and rule. A political party that had been in the forefront of helping the migrants settle in the North East did all it could to keep them as a minority community, so that they would remain a "vote bank" for that particular party.

The result was a fissure in the peaceful diversity of the North East, where one community is now pitted against another for party political gain. This has been happening since the '50s, and there is still an atmosphere of tension and strife.

THE ROOTS OF SEPARATISM

The insurgency movement in the North East is another aspect of the story. The insurgents (or the "terrorists", as the Indian state has proclaimed them) are not against the people or communities (in most cases), they are against the state, especially the Indian state, and against how the seven states in the region came into being, with blatant disregard for the geographical and historical realities of the region.

The emotional root of all insurgency movements in the North East lies in the history of pre-colonial Assam.

The insurgents argue that Assam, or the whole of the North East for that matter, was never part of India proper. The land came to the British after a war treaty between the British forces and the King of Ava in Burma in 1826, what is called the Yandabo Treaty. They argue that, now that the British are gone, and the Kingdom of Ava has disintegrated, the rights to rule over the land revert to the descendents of the Ahom kings, and effectively to the local inhabitants. That the North East is part of the Indian Republic is considered a gross mismatch.

Post-Independence, the Government of India has divided Assam into several states to satisfy the national aspirations of the tribal populations living within the then borders of Assam.

In 1963, the Naga Hills District became the 16th state of India under the name of Nagaland.

In 1970, in response to the demands of the tribal people of the Meghalaya plateau, the districts embracing the Khasi Hills, Jaintia Hills, and Garo Hills were formed into an autonomous state within Assam; in 1972, it became a separate state, Meghalaya.

In 1972, Arunachal Pradesh (the North East Frontier Agency) and Mizoram (from the Mizo Hills in the south) were separated from Assam as union territories; both became states in 1986.

Despite the restructuring of Assam since Independence, communal tensions and violence have remained. Separatist groups began forming along ethnic lines, and demands for autonomy and sovereignty grew, resulting in the fragmentation of Assam.

In 1961, the Government of Assam passed legislation making use of the Assamese language compulsory. It was withdrawn later under pressure from Bengali-speaking people in Cachar.

In the 1980s, the Brahmaputra Valley saw a six-year Assam Agitation triggered by the discovery of a sudden rise in registered voters on electoral rolls. It tried to force the government to identify and deport foreigners illegally migrating from neighbouring Bangladesh and changing the demographics. The agitation ended after an accord between its leaders and the Union Government, which however remained unimplemented, causing simmering discontent.

Since the 1970s, armed separatist groups like the United Liberation Front of Asom (ULFA) and the National Democratic Front of Bodoland (NDFB) have been founded and have grown in strength.

In November 1990, the Government of India deployed the Indian Army, after which low-intensity military conflicts and political murders continued for more than a decade.

In recent times, ethnicity-based militant groups have been on the rise. Regional autonomy has been ensured for the Bodo-Kachari community in Bodoland Territorial Council areas (BTC), for the Karbis in Karbi Anglong and for the people of Dima Hasao District after agitation by the communities because of the sluggish rate of development and the general apathy of successive state governments towards indigenous communities.

These demands for autonomy, for self-rule or complete separation have become more and more fragmented, so that there is currently an armed militant group for every ethnic group in the North East.

IDENTIFYING THE ENEMY

Who is the enemy and who is a friend?

The definition of friendship keeps changing, but the major enemy remains the same: the Indian state. And the state also responded by acting like an enemy. As the demand for independence has grown, since the 1990s, the Indian government has carried out a series of offensives.

Formed in 1979, the United Liberation Front of **Asom** (ULFA) became a force to reckon with in the late 1980s. It virtually ran a parallel government in the state between 1988 and 1990 until the Indian state started two major crackdowns—Operation Bajrang and Operation Rhino. Decades later, the ULFA remains active despite a split in its ranks and the surrender of a large number of its cadres over the years.

The National Democratic Front of **Bodoland** (NDFB) was formed by a group of radical Bodo youth on October 3th, 1986. Like their counterparts in the ULFA, they believe that their nationalities can prosper only if they are outside the Indian state. The NDFB is active in Assam's Bodo-dominated areas bordering on West Bengal and Bhutan.

Manipur is the most difficult case in the North East as far as militancy is concerned. Apart from the fact that there are more militant groups in the state than anywhere else—there are at least seven—the rivalries between these outfits often lead to greater violence. At places, these groups run parallel governments, extorting money or levying "taxes" on people, government officials and businessmen. No transporter can operate in Manipur without having paid off at least three prominent militant groups. Some of the groups, like the Kanglei Yaol Kanba Lup, are attempting to "cleanse" Manipuri society by launching high-profile campaigns against drug peddlers or corrupt government officials and by issuing diktats to "preserve" Manipuri culture.

Nagaland has the oldest running insurgency groups. The Isak-Muivah group of the National Socialist Council of Nagaland (NSCN-IM) is regarded as a mentor by many groups in the North East since it helped form these outfits, nurtured and armed them over the years. But it has created tensions in the North East by demanding a "greater Nagaland" by uniting Naga-inhabited areas spread over other states like Manipur, Assam and Arunachal Pradesh.

In **Tripura**, two major outfits, the National Liberation Front of Tripura (NLFT) and the All Tripura Tigers Force (ATTF) have been on the rampage, killing or kidnapping people with impunity. Tripura, a princely state before Independence, has witnessed a steady decline of its indigenous population, giving rise to militancy among the tribals. Tripura has nearly 10 lakh (a million) indigenous tribals who live in abject poverty in the hilly and often inaccessible areas of the state.

Meghalaya has two active insurgent groups. Arunachal Pradesh and Mizoram are relatively free of militancy, but security experts warn that trouble is round the corner in **Arunachal Pradesh** where the Nationalist Socialist Council of Nagaland—Isak-Muivah (NSCN—IM) is making inroads in some districts. **Mizoram** is perhaps the only state in the region which can claim to have abandoned insurgency. Indeed, the Mizo National Front (MNF), which was underground for 20 years, signed a landmark pact in 1986, came into the open, and now runs the state government.

Following the debate in the Assam State Assembly as to who the Assamese people are, Dr. Dhrubajyoti Bora, an acclaimed novelist and the current president of the Asom Sahitya Sabha, said that those who can read and write the Asomiya language are the Assamese, irrespective of their other identities.

This is a problem that can hardly be solved so easily. Yet Dr. Bora's suggestion might be a good starting point.

Refugees

Sanjukta Dasgupta

Sanjukta Dasgupta is a poet, short story writer, critic and translator, and a Professor of English (and former Head of English and Dean of the Faculty of Arts) at the University of Calcutta.

Dr. Dasgupta's research interests include postcolonial theory and texts, colonial and postcolonial women's writing, migration and diaspora studies, literature and film, women and / in Indian films, translation studies, and creative writing.

So long it had been the *firangis* who did it
But once they went
We do it to our own, for their good

Women, men and children
Ran out of their own homes and land
Seeking refuge in camps

All of them were of the wrong colour
So were their ducks, hens, goats, cows
But they stole their livestock despite the hated colour

Not the timeless war between brand names of Gods
But the seduction for more, instantly some more
Made them puppets of cold-blooded politics

Dazed by the word-jugglers
Long-distance compassion
Misguided efforts

They shot each other on their beloved land
Pathetic puppets with primitive symbols
Sickle, hammer, rods and spears

But in real use
Were rocket launchers, land mines
AK47s and other swanky toys of death

The good earth became a killing field
Neighbours became enemies overnight
Ishwar and Allah were summoned to divide further
Those who had lived in peace so long

Even the refugee camps were invaded
Peace became a tearful prayer for
Refugees in their home places

Those who manipulated the gullible marionettes
Had dreams of conquest
Their capital this time was of course ignorance

Those we thrust into our backyards
They are the ones who pull us back—
The wisdom of the poet's words of long ago

So fearfully distorted
Revised and twisted into a time-serving
Grotesque pastiche, a charade
A nightmare pretending to be a wake-up call!

DIVERSITY WITHIN THE VALMIKI RAMAYANA

Arshia Sattar

Arshia Sattar has a PhD from the Department of South Asian Languages and Civilisations at the University of Chicago. Her translations from the Sanskrit of Tales from the Kathasaritsagara *and* The Valmiki Ramayana *are published as Penguin Classics. She has also written three books for children. Dr. Sattar teaches epic and classical Indian literatures at various institutions in the United States and India and has long been a reviewer of books and a literary critic for various Indian publications.*

I am not going to talk about diversity in the greater Ramayana tradition—A.K. Ramanujan (1991) has already done that. After Ramanujan has spoken, there is very little left to be said. And what he has said certainly cannot be said better. There are Ramayanas, or stories of Rama, in every single Indian language, as well as in the languages of Southeast Asia, even in languages that do not have a script. There are Jain Ramayanas and Gond Ramayanas and Ramayanas in which Rama is a *boddhisattva* [one who out of compassion refrains from entering Nirvana in order to help others—*Ed.*]. Paula Richman's work brings some of this diversity to our attention. She and many others remind us that the Ramayana tradition is as diverse and plural and multi-valent as the many languages and cultures in which it appears—both inside this country and outside. Each Ramayana performance, whether it is the Ramleela from Banaras, or Therakoothu from Tamil Nadu, or Sattriya from Assam, each performance tells a Ramayana that is likely to differ from the one that you and I know, which we think is the only Ramayana, or the best Ramayana, certainly the most "true"

Ramayana. We could not be more wrong. Each Ramayana is true and best for those who tell it.

What we must always hold in our heads and in our hearts is that the Ramayana is not a homogenised monolith, as people around us would now like us to believe. Everyone who chooses to tell the story—and that right belongs to each and every one of us, whether we are women or Dalit or Tamil or Swedish or Kenyan—everyone who chooses to tell the story, will tell it differently. This is a good thing. For it not only enriches the tradition itself, it spreads the story further and wider than any canonical and restricted version can do. For as long as the story of Rama has been around, which is at least 2,500 years, it has been told and re-told, added to, subtracted from, multiplied and divided. For a story that straddles our cultural imagination as well as so much of our cultural expression, a story that gives us metaphors of social control such as the *Lakshman Rekha* [a line not to be overstepped, *i.e.*, strict conventions, specifically for women's behaviour—*Ed.*] and ideas of governance such as *Ramrajya* [an ideal, righteous society based on caste order and duties—*Ed.*], that gives us poetry and painting and music and dance, how could it be otherwise?

It is part of the Ramayana's generosity as a story that it can contain so much diversity within itself, that it can spread itself to include the aspirations and criticisms of so many different kinds of people, that it can bend and sway in response to the music that you want to play, that it can rise in your song, that it can be the landscape of your painting, provide the beat for your dance. It's the only story I know that can do that. And it is this feature of the Ramayana that we should rightfully celebrate and enjoy together.

Having said all this about the greater Ramayana tradition, I want to look closely at what is diverse, plural, questioning, challenging, perhaps even subversive, within the Valmiki Ramayana, which is the oldest Rama story that we have in the world. We believe that the story we call the Valmiki Ramayana was put together sometime between 200 BCE and 200 CE. The next time that we officially hear the story of Rama is when Kamban tells it in Tamil, about 1,000 years later. A lot happens to Hinduism in these intervening centuries. Most importantly, *bhakti* makes an appearance and devotion quickly becomes the central emotion of Hinduism. As you know, *bhakti* was the creed that placed the individual at the centre of the religious experience—how you as a person, whether male or female, Brahmin or

Kshatriya or Dalit, felt about God was more important than any sacrifice or ritual. We are taught that *bhakti* opened up a stratified and hierarchical religion by asserting that God could love everyone, provided you loved him / her back. In a way, *bhakti* made it possible for the Ramayana to proliferate and reflect the aspirations and anxieties of the people that told it.

But let us return to the Valmiki Ramayana for now. Let us examine the story through the lens of diversity, *i.e.*, whether there are different kinds of people / creatures in Valmiki and if there are (and there are), what happens to them. Are there different ideologies in the Ramayana? Are there different ways to live and be that are legitimate and sanctioned? Are there differing codes of conduct that are equally righteous? Or, is there a single dominant ideology to which we must all eventually surrender.

Valmiki tells us the story of a warrior prince, Rama, who, after a series of unexpected and undeserved trials, eventually becomes king. The Ramayana, like the Mahabharata, is essentially a story about warriors, a story set in the universe of the Kshatriyas and concerned with how Kshatriyas can be good Kshatriyas or better Kshatriyas. The values that guide the lives of these men, almost all of them princes, are located in the code for warriors, in Kshatriya dharma. I am going to argue that, in the Ramayana, there are other dharmas, other ways of being, that throw Rama's dharma into relief, as it were, making us and him more aware of what he chooses to do and why he chooses to do it.

Diversity in Valmiki is manifest in the different kinds of dharma, the different ways of being in the world, the different codes of behaviour that its characters live by. Given that there are three kinds of beings in the Ramayana—humans, monkeys and *Rakshasa*s [demonic beings—*Ed.*]—there are also three kinds of ways to be. Further, there are, effectively, three worlds in the Ramayana, each located in and defined by a city: Ayodhya, Kishkindha and Lanka. Each of the cities reflects the nature of the beings that inhabit it, each of them embodies the characteristics of its people. By depicting each of the cities as having a unique milieu, the Ramayana also explores multiple dharmas, or ways of being in the world. Kishkindha, the city of the monkeys, and Lanka, the city of the *Rakshasa*s, are set in contrast to Ayodhya, just as monkey and *Rakshasa* dharmas are contrasted with the human codes of behaviour and ethics lived out by Rama and his brothers. There is, of course, a fourth world in the story, the liminal world of the forest, where different creatures and ways of being collide, where the way one lives and follows dharma appear to be matters of choice. In the cities, however, ways of being and doing are determined and unalterable.

The descriptions of Ayodhya, the city inhabited by humans, are relatively minimal, the city being defined more by references to the nature of its people and the order that prevails in it rather than by its buildings. The most important thing about Ayodhya is the maintenance of order (which includes the four castes behaving as they should) that is consequent upon the righteousness of its rulers and their upholding of dharma. What we see of the city itself is by the way. When the citizens of Ayodhya hear about Rama's coronation, they are delighted:

> [...] the joyous citizens began to decorate the city. Banners and buntings danced in the breeze from the temple spires that gleamed like white clouds, from the homes and terraces of rich and prominent citizens, from roads and city squares, from private homes and public buildings. Even the tallest trees were decorated with brightly coloured flags. [...] Flowers were scattered in the streets, sweet incense filled the air and wooden torches as large as trees lined the streets (Valmiki, *The Ramayana*, transl. Arshia Sattar, 108).

At other moments, as we follow Rama from palace to palace as he hears about and then conveys the news of his banishment, we see the city as a backdrop and we learn that Dasharatha's palace "shone like the peaks of Mount Kailasha".

> Rama looked upon his prosperous city, its squares and highways crowded with horses and elephants and chariots and its people who displayed their abundant wealth, lined with shops displaying goods for sale and he felt proud and happy (121).

While there is wealth and prosperity in Ayodhya, there is an atmosphere of restraint and virtue, of whiteness and purity, of gleaming spires and orderly squares and streets. The only moment of chaos we experience in Ayodhya is when Rama, Sita and Lakshmana depart for the forest:

> As Rama drove out of Ayodhya for his long stay in the forest, the city was filled with the sounds of horses' trappings jingling, of elephants

> trumpeting, of agitated people. The sounds swelled and reverberated as the entire city, old and young, ran behind Rama's chariot as they would run towards water in the parched months of the summer (152).

As an example of the character of the city and the behaviour of its people, in Ayodhya the issue of disputed kingship is resolved with grace and delicacy. Rama does not contest his father's decree that he be banished into the forest for 14 years. His brother Bharata, who inherits the throne as a corollary to Rama's exile, is ashamed of his mother's machinations and tries to persuade Rama to take back the kingship which is rightfully his. He comes to meet Rama in Nandigram, where Rama has decided to live.

> "What will I do with this advice on the duties of a king when I have renounced kingship?" replied Bharata. "The eternally established dharma states that while an older son lives, a younger son cannot be king. Come back with me to prosperous Ayodhya and crown yourself king for the glory of our clan!" (209).

But Rama refuses the throne, and promises to reclaim his inheritance after he has lived out his 14 years in the forest.

The monkeys seem to live a more emotionally charged life in their city of Kishkindha than do the citizens of Ayodhya. As Sugriva, the exiled Monkey King, tells Rama the story of his plight, he refers not only to his brother Bali's power and strength but also to his love of sensuality and drink, and to how Bali claimed Sugriva's wife Ruma even as he reclaimed the kingdom. After Bali's death, Rama cannot enter the city of Kishkindha because of the terms of his exile. But Lakshmana enters Kishkindha after the rains have ended, to remind Sugriva, who has succumbed to the same love of luxury and pleasure as his brother, of his promise to help Rama rescue Sita.

> Lakshmana looked around the city nestling in the valley with its jewel-studded buildings and flower-filled gardens. Full of elegant mansions and shops, Kishkindha overflowed with trees that flowered and fruited all through the year. The monkey citizens were all children of the gods and Gandharvas and they could change their forms at will. They were beautiful to behold in their fine clothes and celestial garlands.

> Kishkindha's roads were perfumed with flowers and sandal paste and the fragrance of natural liquors like mead and toddy wafted through the air. Lakshmana saw the homes of the great monkey chiefs and the wide thoroughfares that gleamed like white clouds. They were decorated with celestial flowers, filled with wealth and grain and adorned by women who shone like jewels. The king's palace rivalled Indra's. It was surrounded by sparkling white walls that were hard to breach. It had several white towers that were like the peaks of Mount Kailasha. Its garden had trees gifted by Indra that gave any kind of fruit you could wish for. They were covered with flowers and provided generous, soothing shade. Mighty Lakshmana entered Sugriva's palace uninvited, as the sun enters a huge cloud. He passed through seven courtyards before he came to the heavily guarded inner apartments that were filled with couches of gold and silver and seats that were covered with rich and beautiful brocades. Lakshmana could hear soft and melodious music when he walked in and he saw scores of women, all of them revelling in their youth and beauty. They sat there, adorned with rare flowers and exquisite jewels, weaving garlands. Lakshmana could not see a single retainer who was lazy, discontented or not fully adorned (355-56).

If Ayodhya is a city of restraint, Kishkindha seems to be a city of pleasure. The monkeys are honourable, but they are also good-looking hedonists who love silks and brocades and jewels and fine liquors. There is a lushness that hangs over Kishkindha and defines the actions of its citizens. The dharma of the monkeys permits the transfer of wives between brothers, and monkey women appear to have freedoms that human women do not. While Tara and Ruma are Sugriva's wives, Tara is also a wise counsellor who advises her first husband Bali and then does the same for Sugriva when he takes her as wife after Bali's death. She is also the one who explains to Lakshmana that Sugriva had not forgotten his promise to Rama, that he had merely lost himself in the pleasures that he had been denied for all his years in exile. It is as if she is making a case for Sugriva to recover himself as a pleasure-loving monkey before he can be of any real use to Rama.

The situation in Kishkindha presents us with an inverted mirror of what has happened in Ayodhya. Again, there are two brothers, one of whom is in exile, and there is only one throne. The Kishkindha dispute is resolved more aggressively when the younger brother (Sugriva) has his older brother (Bali) killed. The grace of Ayodhya has been replaced with violence, with a more visceral solution that is in keeping with the more heightened emotions that motivate the citizens of Kishkindha, whether it is Bali and his anger or Sugriva and his fear. Even Rama has one of his (few) explosions of rage in the Kishkindha region, when he believes that Sugriva has forgotten the terms of their alliance.

The Ramayana reserves its best for last with regard to the cities it describes. It is never more lyrical, never more astonishing in its visual imagery than when it describes Lanka, the island city of Ravana, where virtuous Sita has been imprisoned. Even Hanuman, citizen of Kishkindha, where liquor flows and there are silks and jewels everywhere, is astounded by what he sees in Ravana's city. He is so seduced by its beauty that he almost forgets why he is there.

> Hanuman gazed in wonder at the city of Lanka which seemed like the city of the gods. It had beautiful gateways and ramparts with climbing vines carved on them that surrounded hundreds of mansions festooned with flags and banners. Situated on top of a mountain, the city with its dazzling white buildings looked like it was hanging in the air. [...] Hanuman reached the northern gates and saw the city spread before him like a woman, the walls and ramparts her body, the vast ocean her clothes, the fortifications her hair and the upper stories of the mansions her earrings. Lanka was as fine and lofty as the peaks of Kailasha and seemed to touch the sky. Her tall buildings seemed poised to take off into the air (411–12).

What Hanuman sees when he enters the city is even more wondrous. His experience of Lanka is at night, not in darkness but bathed in a seductive and sympathetic moonlight.

> When night fell, he rose and entered the magnificent city which was divided into quarters by huge, wide roads. Its multi-storied mansions had floors of crystal set in gold and the mansions themselves were studded with pearls and gems [...] Hanuman entered the city filled with lofty mansions that were like autumn clouds [..., he] climbed

onto Lanka's ramparts which were made of precious metals, and stared in astonishment at golden gates adorned with pearls and lapis and diamonds, decorated with beaten gold and silver (413-14).

Hanuman enters Ravana's palace where

> there were thousands of golden vehicles and heavily carved palanquins that shone like the sun. There were vine-covered arbours, opulent rooms, picture galleries, recreation areas with hills fashioned out of wood, pleasant sitting rooms and lavish bedrooms. The palace shone like the sun because of its jewels and because of Ravana's own splendour. Flowing with honey and all kinds of liquor in jewelled vessels, it was like the palace of the God of Wealth (417).

The opulence and excess of Lanka are mentioned over and over again, each image of sensuality and decadence outdoing the one before. And once again, as with Kishkindha, the essence of the city is located in the descriptions of its women.

> Hanuman saw exquisite women who appeared to be high-minded, virtuous and pure. They shone like stars, absorbed in their lovers and their drinking. He saw other women who were illuminated by their own beauty, but they were shy and hid in their lovers' arms, like birds clinging to their mates, enjoying a night of bliss. [...] He saw women with smooth complexions, bare-breasted, with skin the colour of molten gold, others with skin like moonlight. [...] Everywhere he looked, Hanuman saw rows upon rows of moon-bright faces, eyes with long curling lashes and ornaments that glittered like lightning (415).

In Ravana's inner apartments, the beauty and sensuality of the women that Hanuman looks upon increases a thousand fold.

> There were women from the families of royal sages, *Daityas* [another class of demons—*Ed.*], *Gandharvas* [celestial musicians—*Ed.*] and *Rakshasas* and they had all come to Ravana out of love. None had been carried away against her will; they had all been won over by Ravana's personality. None had ever loved another or been the wife of another,

> none except Sita, the daughter of Janaka. Each of Ravana's wives was nobly-born, beautiful, skilled in the arts of pleasure and extremely desirable. And the monkey, who had only worthy thoughts, said to himself, "How lucky Rama would be if his wife was like the wives of this *Rakshasa* king!" Then he grew agitated and reminded himself that Sita was far better than these other women and that the king of Lanka had done a terrible and ignoble thing (421).

Surely Lanka is Ayodhya turned around: fortified strength has become proud decoration, prosperity and wealth have become sensual beauty and showy ostentation, virtue has turned to passion, chastity and restraint into promiscuity and indulgence. These same qualities are displayed in the way Lanka's kingship is sorted out. Once again, Rama is the instrument by which a younger brother acquires a throne. Vibhishana, the younger brother of the king, believes that Ravana is an unrighteous ruler and so he leaves his brother and plots with Rama about how best to conquer Lanka and overcome the might of the *Rakshasas*. His actions are duplicitous, reflecting the secrecy and shadows of the night. Ravana's enormous arrogance will not allow him to return Sita, nor will it let him admit to any mistakes that he might have made. Vibhishana does not fit in this atmosphere charged with excess and immoderation, a spectacular and uncaring decadence that can only be hurtling towards its own doom.

Hanuman's first vision of Lanka is as a woman [Lankini, the spirit of Lanka—*Ed.*]. It is noteworthy that there are no physical descriptions of Ayodhya's women similar to those for the women of Kishkindha and Lanka. While we have some sense of what individual women in Ayodhya (for example, Sita, Kaikeyi, Manthara and Kaushalya) are like, there are no descriptions of Ayodhya's women as a group at all. We are told that Manthara is a hunchback, but the royal women are never described in terms of their physical attributes.

The way women are portrayed is contiguous with the city and the culture / dharma that each of the cities supports. The conservative nature of human relations in Ayodhya is amplified by the fact that the city's women are not described in terms of their bodies or in relation to men. Ayodhya's women are chaste and submissive and stay well within their conjugal boundaries, which makes Manthara's conniving and Kaikeyi's petulant greed all the more remarkable. In Kishkindha, where monkey dharma allows shared sexual partners, women are described in some detail. And finally, in Lanka, where *Rakshasa* dharma allows multiple partners and even abductions, the women are lavishly and lovingly described in all their sensual glory.

Just as human, monkey and *Rakshasa* women have different boundaries in terms of whom they can sleep with, so, too, cities define the possible relations within themselves and offer different solutions to the problems of disputed kingship. It is as if the city is the boundary within which societies can flourish in their unique coherence and with a single dharma in operation, whether it is human society in Ayodhya, monkey society in Kishkindha or *Rakshasa* society in Lanka. It is through these descriptions of the cities and the women that inhabit them that we see how clearly dharma, its maintenance as well as its violation, centres around women, how dharma hovers on the edge of conjugal behaviour and marital transgressions.

While cities can only accommodate one dharma at a time, the forest becomes a space where multiple dharmas can and do exist simultaneously for women as well. We know that the sages' wives inhabit the forest, with their firm adherence to the rules and regulations of marriage and hermit life. But the forest is also the habitat of Shurpanakha, sister to Ravana, who is single and promiscuous. When Shurpanakha approaches Rama and Lakshmana in the Dandaka Forest, she says, "I am the *Rakshasi* Shurpanakha and I can change my form at will. I do as I please, I wander through this forest by myself and strike terror into the hearts of all creatures." She describes her *Rakshasa* brothers and ends her introduction with the boast about her freedom as a single woman, saying that "none of them have any control over me!" (243). As a *Rakshasi*, Shurpanakha has the right to proposition men that she finds attractive, which she does, when she sees Rama and Lakshmana. To the princes, however, this free woman embodies the qualities of the forest itself: wild, unknown, untameable and, eventually, threatening. The rules of Ayodhya, the only rules the princes know, make this single and sexually active woman dangerous. In a terrible miscalculation with far-reaching and devastating consequences, they mutilate the *Rakshasi*, applying the principles of Ayodhya-dharma in a place where it is inappropriate.

In direct contrast to Shurpanakha and all that her presence in the forest implies, there is also the mysterious Swayamprabha, the self-illuminated ascetic who lives in an enchanted cave into which the monkeys stumble as they search for Sita. With the power accumulated through her practice of austerities, Swayamprabha saves the monkey troops and transports them directly to the shores of the ocean. The forest, therefore, supports the sexual aggression and indulgence of Shurpanakha as well as the fierce celibacy of Swayamprabha.

Thus, the forest (or rather, any space outside the city) is an indeterminate space where multiple dharmas can coexist. It is established as a space of fluidity, where shapes can change and where unusual and challenging choices become available. Many scholars have pointed to the fact that in literatures across the world, spaces outside the city are seen as liminal zones, spaces where transgressions can occur without retribution. The rules of the city do not apply, characters come up against the unexpected, the magical and the dangerous. I would like to extend this insight and suggest that when transgressive behaviours or acts (which might have been "allowed" in the forests and in the wilderness) are committed within the city, it leads to disaster. A determined way of life is threatened and quite often shaken. These behaviours have to be contained or uprooted for order to be restored. In Indian texts, these violations and their repair can be read in terms of dharma and its imperatives.

In the case of the Ramayana, these transgressions within the city are catastrophic. The severity of the violations is determined by the nature of dharma in each particular city, but each of the violations involves a woman. Dasharatha's surrender to Kaikeyi's demands goes against the dharma established in Ayodhya, where the norms of behaviour are about restraint and the public good. Bali's addition of Ruma to his harem within the walls of Kishkindha while Sugriva is still alive violates the dharma of Kishkindha, which is otherwise rather more permissive with regard to multiple women and wives. Ravana brings Sita to Lanka by force whereas all the other hundreds of women in his palace have come to him out of their own choice. Any of these actions, from Dasharatha or Bali or Ravana, might have been permissible in the space outside the city, but because they occur within the city, they become transgressive.

We see that there are multiple ways to live within Valmiki's text, that the story itself confronts diversity by showing us that there are different dharmas for different kinds of beings. It also suggests that dharmas can be fluid, depending on who you are and where you are.

The problem is that Rama sets about to kill, literally, these other codes of conduct that nuance the Ramayana. He kills both Bali and Ravana, the king of the monkeys and the king of the *Rakshasa*s, who are arguably, like Rama himself, the upholders and the embodiments of the dharma that their people must live by. He kills them both for acts of transgression with women—Bali for taking Sugriva's wife and Ravana for taking his own. By killing them, Rama imposes human dharma upon people (or creatures) that have other dharmas; who have, for example, other ways of perceiving and treating their women. Already, the Ramayana is flattening out its differences. But the final burial of internal diversity is yet to come.

Let us step back from the story for a moment and look at a few critical determinants that relate to the composition of Valmiki's text. We know that the first and the last books of text that we attribute to Valmiki, the *Bala* and the *Uttara Kanda*s, are later in composition than the middle five books. Clearly, these books were written with *bhakti* and *avatara* theory [incarnation of a deity in a different form—*Ed.*] in the forefront, for it is here that Rama is indubitably God and by extension, in his human incarnation, he is the ideal man, the *Maryada Purushottama*. Rama the man-god returns to Ayodhya and establishes *Ramrajya*, which, apparently, means that everyone knows his place and is very happy. Until one day, a Brahmin comes to his court holding the lifeless body of his son who has died for no discernible reason. Rama sends his spies out into the land and they come back with the news that a Shudra named Shambuka has been practising austerities reserved for Brahmins. This transgressive act has upset the equilibrium of the perfect kingdom and a boy has died because of this disturbance. There is only one solution to restore the delicate balance: the Shudra will have to be killed by Rama himself. Rama finds Shambuka and kills him and immediately the Brahmin's son comes back to life.

After the battle with Ravana, Rama ceases to be a warrior prince and becomes a sedentary monarch presiding over a peaceful and prosperous kingdom. In Valmiki's *Uttara Kanda*, the last book of the epic, Rama entertains Brahmins and listens to their stories. If there are problems here or there, he sends his brothers out to deal with them. Some scholars make the argument that it is this last compositional layer of the Valmiki text that brahminises it, turns it from being a story about a warrior who learns to be a king into a story about a king who is good and noble and just because he bows to his Brahmin advisors and their interests. It is certainly true that the appearance and influence of such Brahmin sages as Vasistha and Viswamitra are most notable in the *Bala* and the *Uttara Kandas*. A 20th-century play in Malayalam, C.N. Sreekantan Nair's *Kanchana Sita* (1961), makes full and fervent use of this hypothesis by portraying a Rama in the thrall of the court Brahmins—so much so that even loyal Bharata is ready to reject the man that king Rama has become.

In the middle books of Valmiki's text, we see Rama trying to eliminate other kinds of dharma. One might say he's busy eliminating diversity itself, by killing those who live differently, who march to the beat of a different dharma as it were. But when we get to the *Uttara Kanda*, it is not simply human dharma that must prevail in Rama's Kingdom and in his story, it is brahminised dharma that has to be established for humans and, one assumes, for non-humans as well.

The diversity and pluralism of the larger Ramayana tradition has been present for centuries and is there for all to see. However, the possibility of individual Ramayanas endorsing diversity and difference within themselves is a slightly knottier problem. Within each Ramayana, Rama seems to work towards establishing a universal dharma that is predicated on the rules by which he himself lives. Nonetheless, there is a Ramayana for each of us; we just have to find it. And if it does not exist, then we have to write it. Let a hundred flowers bloom; the Ramayana tradition and our diverse and pluralistic culture will only be richer for it. Given the times in which we live, perhaps we can be satisfied with a celebration of the fact that there are three hundred Ramayanas, ones that come from different languages, cultures, castes and nations. If we are allowed to even acknowledge these, we will have won a battle in what promises to be a long war.

Religious Fundamentalism and Secularism: With Special Reference to Islam

M.H. Zaffar

Although focused on Islam, this essay by the scholar and writer M.H. Zaffar contains a message for narrow-minded, intolerant members of all religions.

RELIGION AS A CONCEPT

Religion is neither a logico-mathematical nor a scientific concept that could be defined precisely and without any ambiguity; nor is it a physical object whose properties can be delineated and described without any room for controversy; thus there can be no final and commonly agreed upon definition of religion. Like justice, love and beauty, the term "religion" may mean different things to different people. So the answer to the question "What is religion?" can never be simple. The individual assimilates the language of a particular linguistic group at a particular stage of history and along with the language, he or she assimilates the ideology that is woven into the very fabric of the language, so usually the individual remains unaware of the fact that their concept of religion is informed by a particular ideology that gives birth to certain particular models and those particular models happen to be only a few among many other possible models. Synchronically, the semantic field does not only differ from one linguistic group to another linguistic group, but also from one individual to another individual within the same linguistic group, depending upon the relative maturity of the individual concerned. Diachronically too, it differs at various points of linguistic evolution within the same linguistic group.

Within these linguistic parameters, let us propose a definition of the concept for the sake of discussion. Religion is a set of beliefs, values, and practices that form a vision or worldview that is not amenable to any empirical verification. But this is an abstract definition and the moment we attempt to give some content to this abstract formula, we find ourselves immersed in a sea of difficulties. The reason for this is that one's concrete understanding of religious concepts is an essential part of one's basic worldview which, as has already been pointed out, is a product of cultural conditioning. The individual assimilates the interpretations current in his own culture and usually accepts them as true. The very concept of religion differs from culture to culture, but each religion has various aspects and elements that constitute it as a vision or worldview and translate it into a plan of action in various spheres of human life. Now the question as to which of the elements that constitute the foundation of a particular religious tradition are most important, has definitely more than one answer. The answer may vary from one group to another group, belonging to the same religious tradition at a particular stage of history, depending upon their relative socio-politico-economic and spiritual evolution; it may also vary from one group to another group belonging to the same religious tradition but at different stages of history. And it may vary from one individual to another individual, belonging to the same tradition depending upon their relative maturity and spiritual evolution.

FUNDAMENTALISM

Literally speaking, a religious fundamentalist is one who believes in and would like to realise certain principles of a religious tradition which he considers to be fundamental to the tradition. In the opinion of the present writer, a fundamentalist may not necessarily be a fanatic or dogmatic. On the contrary, he might have selected the principles after due comprehension, consideration and critical evaluation. They might be quite broad-based and may have a universal appeal, like the principles of: service to mankind, universal brotherhood, peace, truth, love and *ahimsa* (non-violence). We have a galaxy of religious and spiritually evolved individuals belonging to different religious traditions for whom some of these principles were the foundational principles of their religious creed and consequently the guiding forces of their lives. Thus, the problem is not fundamentalism, but any uncritical, unexamined and dogmatic fixation upon any particular gestalt of religion.

Take the instance of Mahatma Gandhi. He had great admiration for all the religious texts, but at the same time he urged a rational and critical approach to their understanding and interpretation. The Mahatma was a fundamentalist of sorts: remember the incident of his son's sickness when the doctor had prescribed chicken soup for the ailing child. Gandhi risked his son's life but did not compromise on his principles. He believed in the sanctification of all life. "Politics divorced from religion" was for him "a corpse fit only to be burned". For him there was no separation between religion and politics. Truth and *ahimsa* were fundamental principles of Gandhi's creed and all his life, he strived for their realisation, at the cost of his life.

Secularism as articulated in the Indian Constitution implies that religion is a relationship of a personal nature between the believer and God. It leaves the individual and society free for structuring all other spheres: social, economic, political, cultural, *etc.* Secularism also includes religious tolerance. According to this conception, the role of religion is essentially inspirational and spiritual rather than legal and / or institutional. Thus the conception of religion enshrined in the Indian Constitution does not harmonise with Islam as understood by the average Indian Muslim. But there is an urgent need to develop a unified Islamic perspective which would resolve the conflict between the traditional concept of Islam as a complete code of life and the contemporary secular revolution; and, keeping in view the spiritual depth of Islam, this is not an impossible task. But for this, we shall have to re-interpret the basic concepts and values of the Islamic tradition. Jamal Khawaja in *Quest for Islam* (1977) comments:

> The Muslim reservations about secularism and the modern conception of religion as a personal relationship between man and God are perfectly natural and understandable. These reservations should be viewed with sympathy rather than anger or negative despair and at the same time, all efforts should be made by Muslim intellectuals to educate the Muslim mind in its basic task of cultural self-evolution. Muslims as a body must be helped to liberate themselves from a rigid fixation upon

> the mediaeval gestalt of Islam as distinct from its essence as such. They must be helped to realise that while the essence of Islam is eternally valid, no particular interpretation of the basic essence should be regarded as immutable, such that the slight departure from it amounted to disbelief, disrespect or disloyalty to God and the Prophet (*Preface*, xii).

It is this fixation upon a particular interpretation of Islam, this conditioning with a certain inherited model, which creates problems. The uncritical and unexamined acceptance of certain principles as fundamental to a religious creed and an ideologically informed interpretation of these principles make fundamentalism an undesirable phenomenon. Theoretically, the problem can be addressed on two levels: firstly, on the level of choosing and selecting the fundamental principles of a particular religious tradition, and secondly, on the level of interpretation of those principles. How a particular gestalt, a particular interpretation of a religious tradition becomes a dominant one has varied and complex reasons, beyond the scope of the present discussion. Our task is to explore the possibilities of deconstructing the ideologically informed, traditionally inherited and accepted models. Indicating the possible role of vested interest and ideology in the interpretation of religious texts, R.S. Bhatnagar (1992) writes:

> Like all information, religious information can assume the form of a commodity—a commodity which could be withheld, or released partially or in adulterated form, which lends itself to commercialisation (and today its political misuse cannot escape the attention of any serious citizen). The exclusive custody and right to interpret "the word of God" is more or less a monopoly (94-95).

But for perceptive and discerning minds, there are many openings in the prison house of language, although the ideological structures are the hardest to break. Regarding the interpretation and re-interpretation of religious texts, the author further writes:

> It is important to note that we are not saying that the original texts are to be rewritten or can be rewritten. No letter needs to be altered. But this does not imply that the understanding of one reader cannot differ from the understanding of another one [...], yet claims to some favoured

interpretation are institutionalised. Any deviation is frowned upon, nay invites severe indictment (95).

IJTIHAD IN ISLAM

In principle, Islamic Shariah is always open to *ijtihad*, that is, interpretation and deduction of laws in the light of the fundamental principles. We have to comprehend and interpret the Qur'an and Sunnah in accordance with the epistemic level attained by society. At present, there are four Sunni legal schools and one Shia school. But it is a historical fact that there have been many more schools, which became extinct due to politico-historical exigencies. There have been restrictions on *ijtihad* on the part of various rulers to restrict proliferation of these schools and to maintain the status quo. But these restrictions have been purely political and have little to do with the spirit of Islam. Shaykh Aga Buzurg Tehrani (1980-81, published posthumously) wrote:

> Adherence to any *madhhab* (legal school) was not known to Muslims from the time of the advent of Islam up to the period when the four *madhahib* gained currency, and this was after nearly two centuries. But even then, though the concept of *madhhab* had developed among them, the restriction making it obligatory to follow one of the four *madhahib* and proscribing others [...] took place in the 7th-13th centuries at the Caliph's order for political reasons. Otherwise, the ability to deduce the *ahkam* (orders) from the Qur'an and the Sunnah is neither confined to any particular country, nor limited to particular persons to the exclusion of others.

Rejecting the limitation on legal schools or *madhahib* and calling for the revival of *ijtihad*, Muhammad Siddiq Hasan Khan (1879) commented:

> One who limits the grace of God to some of his creatures and confines the ability to understand the sacred Shariah to those of past eras, is guilty of insolence towards God Almighty and His Shariah, which has been laid down for all His servants who adhere to the Qur'an and the Sunnah. If adherence to the Holy Qur'an and the Sunnah is limited to the people of the bygone ages and if there remains nothing for those

> who came after them to do except imitate their predecessors and if they cannot deduce the knowledge of God's law from the Qur'an and the Messenger's Sunnah, what are the grounds of this false distinction and this spurious dogma? (*Husul-al-ma'mul min 'ilm al-usul*, 186, quoted in Buzurg Tehrani, with slight interpolation).

While discussing the concept of *ijtihad*, an early 20th-century writer, Muhammad Farid Wajdi, observed:

> When the Muslims were afflicted by the malaise of social stagnation and affected by the inability to understand the secrets of the Shariah, they took resort in the excuse of the closure of the gates of *ijtihad* and legal inference to conceal their own weakness. The truth is that this door remains open, as affirmed by express statements of the Qur'an and the Sunnah, till the Day of Resurrection (*Da'irat al-ma'arif*, Vol. 3, 197, published *c.*1923-25, quoted in Buzurg Tehrani, with slight interpolation).

Thus it is amply clear that there is no bar on re-interpreting the Qur'an and the Sunnah in accordance with the epistemic level attained by contemporary society, and a systematic conceptual framework can be built that will give rise to an Islamic perspective that will harmonise not only with contemporary knowledge but also with the socio-political realities of the times.

Finally, the writer would like to touch upon briefly the exclusivist claim that has been traditionally made in the name of Islam. Belief in the pre-eminence of the faith cannot be challenged, but that is not the same as exclusivism. Muhammad Legenhausen (1997), a contemporary religious scholar and Muslim convert, explains:

> According to Islam, the correct religion ordained by God is that revealed to the last of His chosen prophets, Muhammad; this and no other religion is required by Allah of all mankind. In this sense, Islam is exclusivist. However, at various times prior to His final revelation, God ordained other religions by means of His prophets. [...] The previous teachings were not incorrect, and they were sufficient to guide the people for whom they were revealed, to salvation [...so] there can be no denying

> that different paths can lead to God, and in different circumstances have been ordained by Him.

Thus while the enemies of Islam (submission to the will of God) will face punishment,

> for those who honestly accept an invalid creed, it must be admitted that this invalid creed itself may be the vehicle through which God extends to them His grace and leads them to salvation.

According to Islam, God's grace is unlimited and there is always room for hope that even those considered most wicked may, by the grace of God, find the way to true repentance and salvation: "And that grace is in the hand of Allah, He bestows it on whom He will and Allah is lord of Mighty Grace" (al-Qur'an 57: 29, transl. by M.H. Shakir).

Church in the Liminal Space—Limitations and Possibilities

C. Joel Gnanadoss Timothy

Joel Timothy is an Assistant Professor in the Department of English at the American College, Madurai.

India is a land of multiple Christianities, and various forms of Christian practices add to the religious pluralism and cultural diversity in India.

As Western Christian denominations have encountered Hindu religious practices, Christianity has been appropriated through a complex process of social, cultural and religious synthesis. Since its arrival on the shores of India, Christianity has undergone many creative mutations. Each strand of Christianity in India competes and contests with the others, creating a rich blend of cultural and religious practices. Christianity has been localised in a few cases; however, in most cases it maintains the Western missionary tradition.

The Church in India has an uncomfortable symbiotic relationship with the Western models. It is neither completely Western nor entirely indigenous. Since the heyday of missionary activity, there have been attempts to "Indianise" the Church in India. In the postcolonial reality, the agenda for contemporary Indian theologians seems to be different from that of the missionary objective. The Church now seems to inhabit a liminal space, with indigenous practices being incorporated into the Western religious paradigms.

I shall argue that, while it is indeed desirable to have Indian varieties of Christianity, it would involve complex processes to de-Westernise the Church without any guarantee of a positive outcome.

I

India's religious pluralism, mysticism and cultural ethos of tolerance are well suited to this kind of cultural transaction. The dilemma, however, is what elements and to what extreme those elements can be made a part of the Church in India. Renowned Indian theologians like Sundar Clarke and Bishop Appasamy have advocated an Indian form of Christian *bhakti* and worship rituals. Bishop Appasamy (Bishop in the Church of South India in the '50s), who is considered the forerunner of indigenous theological thought, confirmed in 1931 at the Sat Tal Ashram founded by Dr. Stanley Jones: "the sharing of our religion with others is becoming possible" (quoted in Francis (ed.) 1992, xii). Appasamy sees a correlation between the devotional *bhakti* tradition in India and the way that St. Paul envisioned Christian discipleship—offering oneself as a living sacrifice. The *bhakta* (devotee) who is the servant of God is required to offer his life in service to God and human beings. Bishop Appasamy also favoured "an order of service which appeals to the best in us as Indians" (quoted in Francis (ed.), 94). At the same time, he avers that not all Hindu rituals can be or need to be absorbed into the Church. Conceptually, Indian spirituality has many theological and devotional aspects to offer Christianity. In practice, however, some Hindu rituals are deemed theologically incompatible with Christian doctrines.

Bishop Appasamy narrates the experience at Bishop's Theological College at Tirumararyur in Tirunelveli District in South India. The special Indian form of Christian worship held at the seminary got the sanction of the Bishop of that diocese. This service included Hindu religious and cultural traditions such as washing of feet before entering the church (signifying purity), silence and *ashtanga namaskara* ("salutation with eight limbs of man"—signifying total dedication to God). Appasamy's narration and analysis give indication to the kind of viable cultural synthesis.

It would be appropriate at this juncture to draw our attention to the architectural design of church buildings that stand testimony to the process of cultural exchange and cultural sensitivity: the Jubilee Chapel at American College (founded in 1881 by the American missionaries) and the more recent Cathedral (belonging to the Church of South India) in Madurai. These serve as examples of cultural rootedness and the Church's ineluctable bond with the Western denominational system. The Chapel at the American College was designed in the Indo-Saracenic style with lofty arches. The dome atop the chapel corresponds to the mosque in the locality. It is believed that the architectural design was an expression of inclusiveness aimed at the large Muslim population in this area.

Stone pillars adorn the exterior veranda of the fish-shaped Cathedral. Each pillar has one of many Christian symbols engraved on it. There is another interesting engraving on each pillar along with a Christian symbol: a cross on a lotus or a lotus at the centre of the cross. The lotus and the cross proclaim that the Church is Indian and that Indian culture has been assimilated into the Church's praxis. Yes, to a good extent. But the validity of this proclamation becomes suspect if the liturgical issues are considered. The fish shape of the Cathedral is also noteworthy as it situates the Christian faith in this region. Significantly, the fish in this context is symbolic on two levels: the fish was the ensign of the ancient Pandyan Kingdom, of which Madurai was the capital city, and the fish was also an early Christian symbol.

The loud pronouncements made by these concrete examples are insufficient to prove that the Church has become Indian. They neglect the fact that deeper, on-going interactions with the local forms continue to happen, resulting in multiplicity of Christianity. As Bishop Appasamy has suggested, an Indian form of worship service is missing in the churches mentioned above. The pattern of worship services in both places adheres to Western denominational patterns. Liturgically, the CSI borrows from the Anglican, Presbyterian, Wesleyan Methodist and American Congregationalist traditions. A cursory glance at the prayer book reveals a Western slant. Though there is an order of service based on Tamil music, it is seldom adopted in any of the services at the Chapel or at the Cathedral. Another notable phenomenon in mainline Protestant churches is the existence of liturgy for observing social customs such as *poopunitha neerattu vizha* (when a girl attains puberty, a "Christian" service at home or a *mandappam,* a temporary temple porch similar to the one in Hindu tradition, is practised among rural and even urban Christians) and betrothal rituals.

Both Catholic and Protestant Church praxis is marked by this ambivalence in their relationship with the Western churches and with local customs. While some local cultural and religious practices pertaining to the life cycle rites have been integrated into the Church, organisationally and liturgically, the Church seems to be set on the firm foundation of Western denominational tradition. As an institution, the Church's attempt to engineer social interaction with other religious groups seems to be "anchored on abstract theological concepts" (Selva J. Raj 2004, 10) that have emerged from the West.

II

Where religious / cultural synthesis is most evident is in laity practices. This, according to Raj, "is a grassroots phenomenon" that "emerges from lived experiences, existential concerns and human / spiritual needs of [Christian] laity and their Hindu neighbours (42). He argues that the festival of St. Antony of Uvari, in the Southeastern region of Tamil Nadu, has become a space of social and religious interaction between Hindus, resident Christians and visiting pilgrims.

> Uvari St. Antony is especially renowned for his powers over demonic spirits, particularly malevolent local Hindu deities / spirits like Isakki Amman [originally from a *devadasi* family, she is considered a "destructive vengeful Goddess" but also a protector of her devotees] and Chutalaimadan [one of the sons of Siva, born from his third eye] (34).

The pilgrims and devotees practise a ritual of food called *asanam*. This includes hair-shaving, ritual sacrifice of goats or chickens, fasting, ear-piercing, feeding 13 beggars or the poor or the destitute, cooking and offering *pongal* (a rice dish) and a ritual purificatory bath. Raj tries to prove how the Catholic festival at the shrine of St. Antony is the locus of Hindu-Christian social / religious interactions. Some of the devotional exercises mentioned above still form part of the Catholic laity practice in their own parishes. The pilgrimage to Vellankani Shrine often entails most of these acts.

These acts of piety express various beliefs and emotions: thanksgiving, promise, petition, *etc.* The same religious assumptions and beliefs undergird Hindu and Catholic practice, with the difference being only in the deity / saint worshipped. The devotional elements are anti-structural and hence conducted outside the church, that is, not during the regular worship service. The Catholic leadership does not condemn these laity practices. Another Catholic tradition that finds a parallel in the Hindu tradition is the procession of the deity / saint on a *chapparam* (sacred cart) during church festivals. The Tamil Roman Catholic Church, in keeping with the Vatican Council II decree, has shown a readiness to acculturate with local practices. In a speech to the participants of the national congress of the Movimento Ecclesiale di Impegno Culturale, on January 16th, 1982, Pope John Paul II highlighted the issue thus:

> The synthesis between culture and faith is not only a requirement of culture, but also of faith [...]. Faith that does not become culture is not fully accepted, nor entirely reflected upon, or faithfully experienced (quoted in Valiyakunnel 2013, 2).

On the other hand, among the Protestant laity in Madurai (also the rest of Tamil Nadu) the principle of differentiation seems to be at work. Since the Protestant Christians believe that Hinduistic practices are heathen and that assimilation corrupts the original Christian faith, they are disinclined to the idea of accommodating Hindu religious practices. Hence, in terms of worship rituals, they align with European / American denominational paradigms. Some Christians refrain from eating the delicacies prepared during Hindu religious festivals such as Deepavali, Pongal, Vinayaga Chathurti and Navarathri for fear that they might have been offered to Hindu gods and goddesses as part of *pooja* (worship). Some consider visits to temples as sacrilegious acts. These two examples underscore the attitude of differentiation found among the Protestant laity.

However, on the social level, Protestant Christians seem not to show much restraint when it comes to incorporating practices that pertain to life cycle rituals. In arranged marriages, after the man and the woman have agreed to marry each other, women from the groom's side will visit the bride in her house and place jasmine flowers on her hair. This ceremony is called *poovaithal*. Though it is not mandatory, it is a confirmatory action before the betrothal carried out by the groom and his family members.

III

The fact that Christianity in India is diverse is further adduced by *adivasi* / tribal Christianity. This strand presents to us a paradigm for Christian practices. The *adivasi* group is diverse and spread across India. A large group of *adivasis* in the North Eastern region of India have embraced Christianity. The tradition of the Mizo-Christian community in India provides a notable example of how local cultural practices can be incorporated into the Church. Mizos have been converted to Christianity through the missionary activity of Baptists, Catholics, Lutheran and Anglican mission groups.

Change of religion is definitely an alienating experience, particularly for these close-knit tribal communities. Conversion means isolation from the *adivasis*' own communities and their beliefs. Religious and social practices are so deeply interwoven into *adivasi* culture that change of religion means self-imposed ostracisation. But since the revivals in 1906, there have been attempts to integrate some Mizo practices into Christian worship. In the words of Leonard Fernando and Gispert-Sauch (2004):

> [*Adivasi* churches are at the] stage of recovering the basic myths of each tribe in the light of their faith in Christ. There is also a conscious effort to stress the importance of symbols in the primeval world, offering a perception of the faith differently and in some senses richer than that which comes from concepts (217).

This observation succinctly encapsulates how religious synthesis can produce localised forms of Christianity.

By the 1920s, hymns set to Mizo tunes started to appear. These hymns may be described as "Mizo-Christian Hymns". They are neither wholly Mizo nor Western, but are "adaptations of Mizo singing to the strictures of Western hymnody". Fernando and Gispert-Sauch record that drums are a common sight at Revival meetings and church worship. They also observe that during the revival in 1906, there was "stamping on the floor" similar to Khasi dance. Even now, it is common to see some inspired worshipper dancing in front of the altar in spiritual ecstasy. Initially, it was objected to by the missionaries due to its pagan nature. According to Pachuau, "a major contribution of the revivals [...] was its influence on the interweaving of Christianity and Mizo cultural ethos" (quoted in Fernando / Gispert-Sauch, 215). When the church integrates itself to the local tradition what happens is "the celebration of cultures for their life-giving values and [...] the transformation of (challenge to) values which are life-negating" (quoted in Michael 2009, 81).

The interaction between Christianity and the *adivasi* worldview offers scope for fresh theological perspectives. In the tribal consciousness there is space for harmonious coexistence of human and nature. Human beings are conceived as part of nature and not outside of it. Ecological Theology is a result of this dialogue between the two. It may have strong connections with the tribal expressions of Christianity elsewhere in the world. It is less popular and polemical than Dalit Theology. The focalisation of Christianity through the *adivasi* perspective and cultural symbols may prove counter-discursive to the capitalist and exploitative discourses.

IV

The Church's engagement with the caste question showcases yet another duality. Caste in the Church functions both as a cultural signifier and for political convenience. Caste is ubiquitous in the Church. The Church is not untouched by its presence. Down the centuries, the Christian faith as practised in India has been at variance with cultural formations of caste and gender. Caste continues to manifest itself in many subtle ways within the Christian community and in the Church. That caste dynamics surface during Church elections and in matters of appointments to various positions reveal the extent to which caste is seen as an integral part of the Church. Whereas incorporation of some Hinduistic rituals "on the ground" is condemned as unchristian and heathen, the discriminatory practice of caste, which is violative of the Christian doctrine of equality of all humans in the sight of God, is intricately woven into the structure of the Church. In much the same way, cultural assumptions about gender are reinforced and naturalised through the Church's practices.

The ethnographic colonial state viewed caste as endemic to India and also as a means to understand the social fabric of India. The missionaries who lived during the time of the East India Company and in the colonial period confronted this reality and conducted socio-cultural experiments involving caste and Christianity. The main agenda for the missionaries, both Catholic and Protestant, was proselytisation. Some missionaries like Robert de Nobili neatly segregated the external realm of rituals and the inner core of spiritual experience of salvation. De Nobili was a Jesuit priest who came to Madurai in 1606 and settled in Pudur, Madurai. His "accommodation strategy" is an "active incorporation of Christian centres into a local political system" (Mosse 1994, 89). He did not reject caste. Rather, he used caste as a means to spread Christianity. De Nobili's soteriological belief was that the content was more vital than the form, the faith than the expression of it. Caste was only an external feature that did not interfere with the personal experience of salvation.

De Nobili considered Brahmins to be representatives of the Hindu world and believed strongly that by reaching out to the Brahmins, he could take the Gospel to the whole of Hindu society. So he chose to imitate the Brahmin lifestyle in order to entice them to Christianity. He built a mud hut in a Brahmin quarter, took off his black soutane and wore an ochre robe, ate one vegetarian meal a day, and inscribed himself into the caste hierarchy by proclaiming that he was a *kshatriya* (since he hailed from an Italian noble family). He encouraged the creation of an Indian clergy, based on Sanskritic tradition and developed two classes of Christian priests—Brahmin *sanyasis* and the *pandarasamis*. The former catered to the spiritual needs of the Brahmins and upper castes and the latter shepherded the lower castes. The *pandarasamis* played effective roles not only as priests but as middlemen between the Church and the local caste chiefs. De Nobili's ingenuity at cultural synthesis allowed the display of caste markers such as the Brahmin *kudumi* (hair tuft) in the church because he believed that that did not really hamper personal faith.

The cultural ethos of that period forbade the upper castes and the lower castes to worship in the same building. This problem was "resolved" by assigning different spaces to different castes in the church. The upper castes were allowed to occupy the nave and the lower castes were made to sit on the horizontal side wings in the cross-shaped church.

In Sivaganga District, near Madurai District, Brahmins participated in the Eucharist before the Dalits, thus avoiding their polluting touch. The Protestant churches in and around Madurai encountered the same problem. In fact, caste was one of the issues the early Protestant missionaries, particularly the missionaries from the American Madura Mission, found difficult to reconcile with Christian doctrines. The CSI Whitin Memorial Church at Pasumalai, a place of intense Congregationalist American missionary activity in Madurai, was renovated in 2003. In this process, it seems to me that the horizontal wings allocated to Dalits were made to disappear in a symbolic merger with the centre. But Dalit Christians continue to be discriminated against in many other ways within the Church, irrespective of their denominational affiliation.

According to Mosse, the accommodation strategy of Robert de Nobili had many consequences. In the village of Alapuram, now in Ramnad District, the cult of Saint James was, in the 17th and 18th centuries, an important Church festival. St. James, or *Sandiyakappar* in the local parlance, was the saint of the miraculous banyan tree. This Church festival was patronised by the Hindu king and also by the local Maravar chiefs. The saint himself was portrayed as belonging to the Maravar caste (warrior elite) and as the protector of the village. These chiefs met the expenses for "lighting, incensing and other religious worship". The extent to which Hindu practices and caste practices were imbibed by the Church could be known by the fact that religious gifting, Church honours (*kovil mariyatai*) and festival sponsorship (*mantakapadi* system) replayed the Hindu temple festival tradition with its caste regulations. In a place called Sarugani, Mosse records, the image of the Risen Christ would be taken on a huge platform on a *ter*, or temple cart. The prestations of Cloth and Betel Nut would be given by the presiding Catholic priest. The upper caste Catholic donors would receive the honours from the high-caste Catechist from inside the church and the service castes on the steps of the church. Until 1960, the "Catholic Untouchables" were excluded. There is a peculiar dilemma that can be seen in the anthropological examples cited by Mosse and in contemporary Church praxis. Christianity in India seems to reject Hindu rituals as pagan, as originating from the Devil himself. For the early missionaries, as well as for the neo-charismatics and mainline Protestant and Catholic churches, salvation has always meant a rejection of Hindu practices. Yet, ironically, on the question of caste, the Church and its pious members silently, and in most cases vociferously, defend it by allowing it to surface. While some Christians see the gods and goddesses of Hindu religion as devils incarnate, they continue to maintain the evil practice of caste within the Church and in society. An attitude of selective differentiation from the local cultural religious practices is thus evident in the Church. In matters of the "spiritual" domain, that is, in matters relating to the salvation of the soul, the Church and the laity alienate themselves from the local groups. But in matters relating to social issues, Christians seem to justify certain practices.

Mosse's study presents us with the question of "Christianity accommodating caste or caste accommodating Christianity?" The casteist worldview and practice in the Church is far from over. Conversion to Christianity does not take away the sting of stigma nor does it promise constitutional rights / security for Dalit Christians. The category of Dalit Christian falls out of the scheme of the affirmative policies enshrined in the Constitution. They are neither accepted as equals to other Christians within the Church nor are they beneficiaries of the government's policies. Even many years after converting to Christianity, the tag "rice Christians" continues to frame their lives. This is a pejorative term used to describe Dalit Christians which insinuates that they converted to Christianity for material benefits and not out of any spiritual urge or of their own volition. Neither conversion nor reservation seems potent enough to remove the stigma from the Dalits.

The presence of Dalits in the Church has led to the rise of Dalit Theology. It emerged in the 1980s and has contributed positively to the already complex Indian expression of Christianity. With its strong roots in the Dalit movement of the 1960s and 1970s, Dalit Theology is the response of this marginalised group to the Christian message. It underscores equality and dignity of all people. Dalits oppose the idea of the indigenising of Christianity. For they argue that indigeneity is nothing more than the Brahminic-Sanskritic tradition existing in the Church. The attempt to re-interpret the Bible from a Dalit vantage point has opened up possibilities for new forms of amalgamation that are sensitive to the subaltern sub-cultures. With its central focus on justice for Dalits, who continue to be discriminated against in the Church, Dalit Theology has revolutionised the theological thinking in India. The discourse of Dalit Theology was inaugurated by leaders from Protestant churches. They include Arvind Nirmal, James Massey and K. Wilson. Dalit Theology is part of what has come to be known as Third World Theology and it is similar to the Liberation Theology of South America and the Minjung Theology that developed in Korea. However, Dalit Theology to a large extent has remained locked up within seminaries, receiving institutional support from the Tamil Nadu Theological Seminary in Madurai, the United Theological Seminary in Bengaluru and the Gurukul Theological College in Chennai. It has not been able to influence the praxis of the Church. The Church itself seems to have been caught up inevitably in caste politics.

V

In summary, we can say that the Church in India is a site of dialogic process, the locus of socio-cultural, religious interactions and intermingling. It is an interstitial, amorphous place of constant negotiation and new formations. Rather than looking at it ruefully, we need to look at this position of the Church in India as one of many possibilities and of fruitful cross-fertilisations. In India, religious identity is highly politicised. Inculturation without a strong commitment to social justice will further marginalise the already marginalised. As Christianity grows in India and encounters the local traditions, it must not also be seen as an alien religion. The Church must be positive in its attitude towards other religions and it is worthwhile at this point to recall the then Cardinal Joseph Ratzinger's view: "We should no longer speak of inculturation but of the meeting of cultures or 'interculturality'" (quoted in Valiyakunnel 2013, 4). While it is acceptable and to an extent permissible to have "the dialogue of rituals", "the lived and living ecumenism of the laity", "the dialogue in action" (Raj, 42), it is dangerous and unchristian to embrace and uphold caste ideology even in the subtlest form. Discriminatory practices on the basis of caste, gender, class and sexuality are to be considered even more unchristian than some Hinduistic practices rejected by pious Christian communities. The Church in India at present is also at a theological and moral crossroads. In order to be relevant in contemporary society, it must be alive to the social realities. Otherwise, there is a danger of self-alienation.

The Visit

Gayatri Pagdi

Gayatri Pagdi is an author, editor and translator, who has been published in the South Asian Literary Review *and has written books on history, culture and current affairs. Her translations include biographies of Narendra Modi and Dr. Ambedkar and the poetry of Dalit poet Heera Bansode, for which she received an acknowledgement from the Sahitya Akademi in 2007. She is also a researcher in the field of Spirit Communication.*

Last week, a priest from the church came to our house as promised by Mrs. Grace D'souza. She had met my mother one day and had said that she knew someone who would like to pray for Praveen, my husband, who was ill for long. So was it okay if he came over?

"Of course!" my mother said.

So the priest came to our home. I wasn't sure what to call him. Should I call him "Father"? He was of my age. Then "Sir"? Did people call priests "Sir"? "Mr." would sound rude. So I only said "Hello". Mrs. D'souza couldn't make it, but there was another lady who accompanied the priest. She wore a peach-coloured saree.

He went to meet Praveen in our room. Meanwhile, there was chaos in the kitchen. We usually offer milk, with milk-masala added to it, to all holy people who come to our house. My mother started filling up a glass of milk.

My sister was shocked. "He is a Christian priest! How can you offer him what you offer a sadhu?" she asked.

"Why?" my mother was innocent.

"Look," my sister said, "He's Christian. They don't drink such things. You have to give him wine."

"Wine? Now where will we get wine from? And why wine?"

"They are Western in their ways. Western religious people don't have milk."

"He is not Western," my mother said. "He lives 20 minutes away from our house."

"That doesn't matter," my sister said. "Will we offer milk to an Imam?"

"Then, what else will we offer? Dates from Arabia?" My mother was irritated.

I wasn't sure. I was the source of all this confusion. The priest had come to see Praveen, so I felt responsible.

"We have wine," I said, uncertainly.

"I don't know what to do with wine. You girls manage," my mother said and went out of the kitchen.

I felt totally at a loss and disgusted with myself. I had no knowledge of world etiquette.

"Now, just a minute…" my sister took charge. She's good at organising things related to social occasions. "Let's look at the wine. What wine is it?"

My niece had already pulled out the wine bottle. It had been lying in the fridge for years now, along with pickles, chutnies and *murabba* (fruit preserve). "It's green," she said.

"*Green* wine? There's no such thing. There's either red or white," my sister frowned.

"The bottle is green," I explained to my niece. As for what kind of wine it was, I didn't know. It had French words on it. You don't just generally give wine to people at 4 in the evening. Do you?

I didn't know.

My mother came in. "Are you really giving him that wine? It's a very old bottle. Who knows who got it and when… Just check the expiry date."

"Wines don't expire. The older they are, the better they are supposed to be. But you have to give them in special glasses. These *sarbat* (sherbet) glasses won't do."

I felt weepy. What had I got these people into? Now wine glasses…from where?

And with wine, what? Only wine? You don't give only tea to people. You offer something else with it too.

Puffed rice?... No!

Biscuits? I wasn't so sure.

My sister saw my face and said, "You keep out of this. We don't want you to break down at this time."

"Sometimes they have wafers in the church," my niece suggested, helpfully.

"Go, run..."

"I'll get Lays. What flavour?"

"Any."

"Don't get onion flavour," my mother said. "Nobody eats onion in Shravan."

"They don't have a month called Shravan."

"Chilli? With red flakes in it?"

So, the priest was to get green wine and chilli wafers.

I broke into a sob.

"Everything is under control," my sister said.

The wine bottle had a cruel cork. It just wouldn't open.

"Poke a knife, in it. At least make a small hole..." I advised my niece who was struggling with it. She would be late to buy the wafers.

"You get a different kind of opener for such corks," my sister was appalled at our mismanagement. "You can't just push knives in it. It's of no use."

"The bastards! Who made such corks?" I said, violently.

"Stop abusing," my mother was angry. "A holy man has come to our house. You can't abuse like that. What will he think if he hears this? Call up your doctor and take some medicine. You have started getting hysterical again."

I fell into a chair.

My father came in. "He seems like a nice boy," he said of the priest. "His uncle used to live in Hyderabad, it seems. That place is very close to our house there...Aren't you offering him anything?"

"Yes, tea," my mother said. "These girls have a lot of different ideas but I am going to offer him tea."

"Yes, yes..." my father said. "Add ginger to it. It's raining."

Meanwhile my niece came back with wafers.

"Hmm… good tea," the priest said. "How your body clock reminds you that it's tea time!" he laughed.

He didn't have the wafers of chilli flavour. "Just tea. I don't eat anything at this time."

"We get our tea from the tea shop in Matunga," my mother offered a piece of information.

"Ohh…okay! The one near the station? The next time I'm there, I must pick up some," the priest said.

Three Poems

Peer Khan

Peer Khan is a discreet pen-name, used by this writer only for poetry. Khan is presently working on a sequence of sonnets reflecting the diversity of India, its complex relationship with the English language, and, as in the first poem, aspects of the erotic in an Indian context (note how, in describing his lover's clothes in English, he has to use words that are of Indian origin).

The final line of the third poem references the famous Milton sonnet ending "They also serve who only stand and wait".

DIFFERENT BUT PERFECT

How were you dressed today? I can't forget
Those dungarees—cut short to show the thighs—
You wore for housework, so that (just a bit)
I would have liked to take you by surprise,
There, on the sofa! For your shopping trip
You chose a chintzy outfit and a shawl,
Of calico, I think, and you let rip
With a bright red bandana—at the Mall
All eyes were on you. *Every* style is right:
Seersucker for a picnic on the lawn;
Kashmir pyjamas laid out for the night
(More to be *taken off*, than to be *worn*)—
Different but perfect, whether night or day.
I wouldn't have you any other way.

DANCER

Her steps are tiny for such giant feet,
Although they're "giant" only when they're still.
And *still* she never is. Each move, complete,
Segues the movement after it, until
Past, present, future merge into a blur
Of furious, cold delight and gleaming hair.
After the dance was done I spoke to her—
Though heaven knows what I was doing there.
Another owned her, that was clear to see.
With eyes downcast she barely met my glance.
Relieved to escape my questioning, she
Was happy when they called her back to dance.
And so she whirled, and stamped the boards, and trod.
The God was in her. She was in the God.

STUDENTS

Faces turned upwards, like the thoughts they dream,
They sit transfixed by Teacher till the break.
She holds their future in her hands. They seem
Like helpless rabbits skewered by a snake.
Salwared or sareed, turbaned, light or dark,
A generation waiting to be called
To serve their country (and themselves), they mark
Professor Gupta's every move, enthralled.
The lesson that they learn is this: to wait,
To take it step-by-step, and patiently.
India needs them. It is not too late—
The door is closed, but Teacher has a key.
They must be small, who one day would be great.
They also learn who only sit and wait.

Voices of Dissent in Maharashtra

Ramu Ramanathan

Ramu Ramanathan is a playwright, director and editor based in Mumbai, a city that he both loves and loathes.

He admits: "I have perhaps penned more plays than I should have," and when asked about the publication of a volume of eight of them, joked that he had no idea what the book would achieve, except that it might increase the number of PhD theses on Indian English theatre.

Once Upon a Time It Is Now. And in the Now I want to tell you a Story. Please do pay heed to this story.

It is a real story with twists and turns.

It has songs and dance.

It has a *tamasha* (a traditional folk theatre show in Maharashtra, which includes dance and songs) and a *powada* (a ballad).

It has action. But by and large, it is about inaction.

It is about justice and injustice.

And finally, since we live in strange times, this tale has *no* happy ending, *nor* winners.

If you look hard enough, you may find a moral in this story.

But to understand it, rule number one is: pay attention.

Rule number two: stay awake.

So...

Once upon a time and the time is sort-of, now, there is a Rashtra.

Some call it the Maha Rashtra.

To imagine Maha-Rashtra as a real place is to miss the point.

Everything is invented, manipulated, shadowy—and a show; a well-choreographed performance.

Those in power are not in power. And those out of power wield it best.

Knowing all this, the Kabir Kala Manch Defence Committee meet the Maha Maharaja of the State in his home-cum-office at Varsha, in 2012. Our agenda: to request his government to withdraw false charges against the Lok Shahirs (people's poets) from the Kabir Kala Manch, and ensure them the right to perform.

The security is polite. The Maha Maharaja is a statesman. Pleasantries are exchanged. Tea and *poha* (a savoury snack made of flattened rice) are served.

Anand Patwardhan boots up his Apple Mac and showcases excerpts from his documentary *Jai Bhim Comrade* on a white-washed wall. On screen, Sheetal Sathe and her co-members of Kabir Kala Manch mobilise audiences in the name of Ambedkar and Phule. There are some sharp witticisms about the abject poverty and slum discontentment. The 15-minute screening is concluded with the following song:

Angrez aaya, machine laya, mil banaya, zhopad patti
Chamar, bunker lohar mehnat, sab samaya zhopad patti

(The British came, brought their machines, made the mills and the slums
Cobbler, weaver, ironsmith, the dregs of our society live in the slums)

The song culminates with the lines:

Gora jake aaya kala, toota woh sapno ka manzar
Sath saalon mein chuna laga hai
Sath saalon mein chuna lagake bikti reh gayi zhopad patti

(The white man exited, the dark-skinned took over,
the land of dreams, collapsed.
The slums got a first coat of primer in seven years,
In seven years, the slums were cheated and put on sale)

For one nano-second, there is darkness.

The Maha Maharaja returns to his seat; the meeting with the leading lights of the defence committee is re-convened.

The point is made: the state should promptly withdraw charges against Deepak Dengle and Sidharth Bhosale and also Sheetal Sathe, Sagar Gorkhe, Sachin Mali and Ramesh Ghaichor.

Above all, that artistes be granted the permission to perform.

The Maha Maharaja agrees that human rights are meant to be defended. Then we chit-chat about the proliferation of Naxalism into urban centres in the State, and how it should be curbed in a humanitarian way. This goes on for 35 minutes.

Promises are made. We exit.

Time passes.

A bit slower for the members in jail, and for those outside on bail.

Meanwhile the official record of the above meeting with the Maha Maharaja goes missing.

The game is afoot.

There are other mini-skits in the other power-corridors. We hear stories of another Maha Maharaja in the cabinet who is casteist, and yet another who abuses all and sundry.

There's a story about one who is surrounded with a raft of telephones, none of which is connected. On these phones, this particular Maha Maharaja conducts Jean Cocteau-type monologues to no one in particular. But we, the people in front of him, applaud him for his prompt support.

Meanwhile the court hearings continue. Inside a bleak-looking Sewri Court. The security is humongous and they keep a strict vigil. One day, the judge does not turn up. On other days, the legalese and the administrative wrangles seem insurmountable. Plus, there is the lack of funds to mount a serious challenge.

As the saying goes, time passes faster, backwards...

Documentary filmmaker Anand Patwardhan adds: "KKM members are Dalits from poor families who do not carry weapons. Their crime is they sing songs. Had a mainstream musician sung the same songs or uttered the sentiments through songs, I doubt the State would have branded them Naxalites and forced them to go underground."

The long arm of the State is now reaching out at KKM family members like Sheetal Sathe's mother, who has lost her job at the Ruby Hall Clinic in Pune, where she worked as an assistant, "due to the 24/7 scrutiny of the State".

It's become a matter of desperate survival.

A PORTRAIT OF KABIR KALA MANCH

Kabir Kala Manch appeared on Pune's theatre scene in 2002. This is the once intellectually proud city that now practises an indifference to politics. The group members sang songs and staged agit-prop plays. They repudiated aesthetics for politics of the stage.

In February 2005, Kabir Kala Manch members got a crash-course in radicalism in the form of the heavyweights of the "Vidrohi Movement" like Bharat Patankar, Kishore Dhamale, Kishore Jadhav, Dhanaji Gurav and Sudhir Dhawale.

The Vidrohi Chalwal in its heyday was a disingenuous counter-code to the mainstream. The mainstream Sahitya Sammelan was held at Mumbai's Shivaji Park. It doffed its hat to Bal Thackeray, Manohar Joshi (then chief minister of Maharashtra) and the Shiv Sena, while the Vidrohi Sammelan hosted in Dharavi was the literature of the Dalits, Muslims, workers and women. While the main meet was funded by the Shiv Sena–BJP government, the parallel meet was self-funded.

The main *sammelan* was a meet of people with *shendi* (hair knot) and *janva* (religious thread), the parallel *sammelan* was that of people with *lathi* (stick) and *ghongdi* (a rough, blanket-size cloth). While the main *sammelan* served *upma* (a savoury snack made of semolina) and *sheera* (a dessert made of sugar, semolina and butter) (publicised on the front page of most Marathi newspapers), the Vidrohi Sammelan served beef and pork. The Vidrohi fine-tuned their tradition to mock.

They protested in front of the World Social Forum in 2004, and pooh-poohed it as the "social world's forum".

Kabir Kala Manch's "mission" became an acquired taste. The arresting language which its urban *shahirs* (singer-poets) belt out, tackle themes like anti-superstition, gender equality and education, and have the usual appeal of that which is deemed street theatre.

HOW ART BECAME ILLEGAL

Shahir Sambhaji Bhagat (a poet and political activist) who mentored the group says: "Kabir Kala Manch is a talented group made up of young Dalit boys and girls. They sing political songs. But they also combat social evils and promote inter-caste marriage." He points out how Sheetal Sathe and Sachin Mali had an inter-caste marriage, for which there was a lot of opposition.

Bhagat continues: "Ambedkarites are today's bad boys in Maharashtra. All that we say or do is under surveillance." Bhagat, also known as "Maharashtra's Gaddar", knows what he is talking about. His play, *Shivaji Underground in Bhimnagar Mohalla*, has run into a spot of bother with the State. The play, which had had more than 200 stagings in Mumbai and Pune, was denied a show in Parbhani Zilla Parishad and likewise in Sangli, because of its "provocative content."

Bhagat says, "We refused to show the script to anyone and went ahead with the show. The response was stupendous. Today, this is the problem with theatre in Maharashtra. Gratuitous art is the norm. Anything other than that means indictment either from the State or from angry demonstrators."

The play has a simple intent, *i.e.*, to re-claim Chhatrapati Shivaji from a militant right-wing mascot to being "a Raja of the Shudras" and highlight his administrative abilities. The musical play, directed by Nandu Madhav (who plays Harishchandra in *Harishchandrachi Factory*), transpires in the here and now.

The plot is as follows: Shivaji is no more and while Yama is escorting his *atma* (soul) back to Swargalok (heaven according to Hindu religious philosophy), he goes missing. The musical piece performed by 17 farm workers from Jalna frequently lacks narrative coherence which it makes up with a pastiche of the absurd, and focuses on who owns Shivaji and why. This is a dense biography of Maharashtra's tallest warrior king and, in spite of the occasional *powada* thrown in as dramatic device, no historical liaison is left unexplored to its furthest implication.

Bhagat says he had a lot of misgivings about staging the play since it would be denied a genuine run of shows due to its "Jai Bhim" tag.

Unsurprisingly, the play has become "a critically acclaimed hit"; and that has muddled the plot.

As Sunil Shanbag, a veteran Mumbai-based director who has grappled with all types of theatre censorship, says: "Maharashtra is well endowed with methodologies and means to prevent plays that irk the State's peace of mind." So on the one hand, the Culture Department and its cronies will say the show must go on, come what may. On the other hand, there are the permissions and NOCs and clearances from the state office cultural secretary; NOC from BMC after paying venue charges and deposits; BMC Show Department's NOC; fire brigade NOC; PWD electrical and stage compliance report; collector Mumbai for entertainment tax clearance after pre-payment of entertainment tax; police station NOC; RTO NOC; RTO bandobast charges; DCP Zone; Rangbhoomi permission for script and lyrics; censor board clearance; police station permission in the ward; and 33 other licenses.

The point is, no other state in India is so empowered. This means, the State can declare every single live performance "illegal" on a technicality.

This is the main reason why Maharashtra has witnessed a longish saga of "banned" plays: *Keechak Vadh* by K.P. Khadilkar, *Sakharam Binder* and *Gidhade* by Vijay Tendulkar, *Mee Nahuram Boltoy* by Pradeep Dalvi, *Bedtime Story* by Kiran Nagarkar, *Yada Kadachit* by Santosh Pawar, *Avadhya* by C.T. Khanolkar, *Golpeetha* by Suresh Chikhale...

The list is endless.

For some opaque reason, there's a cry from certain quarters to include *Shivaji Underground*...in this list.

None of the rules make sense anymore. There's overt clampdown; furthermore, there's covert clampdown.

Consider what is happening in Maharashtra to *tamasha* ...

NO TAMASHA THIS SEASON

A small *powada*, in English. This *powada* is in honour of the lost art of *tamasha*, which highlights why a people's art form is in shambles.

It is called: *No Tamasha This Season.*

No *tamasha* show this season
Says the veteran *tamasgir* (performer) to me

Tomorrow it's Dashehra
Followed by Diwali
The rice, it's peaking
The rains are ceasing
But no *Dholkicha Phad* (touring shows with a special percussion instrument) this season

Seven months of silence
210 dreary days
210 lonely nights
No sound of the applause, no razzmatazz of lights

150 theatre companies, they fold the travelling tents
They iron their costumes, they tune their instruments
They tell their children about ideal prognostications
Of how *tamasha* performances entertained the nation

That was then
This is now
Eighty *jatras* (folk theatre plays)
300 performances
No *suparees* (invitations to perform)
No encores for now
No *tamasha* show this season
Says the veteran *tamasgir* to me

The numbers don't lie
He unwinds his *pagdi* (turban)
Our artistic reputation can't grow
Due to inconsistency of cash flow

There are no yearnings
Therefore, no earnings
Plus, there's a no-show
From 9 p.m. to 5 a.m., my friend
A court ruling that bans us after 10

Unemployed are the artistes
Female dancers and singers
All of whom migrate to gambling dens
Where women are paid more than men

We pay money to the wealthy *sahukaars* (moneylenders)
We pay for the diesel, we pay for the car

We pay for rentals, we pay for the hiring
We pay for taxes, we pay for complex licensing

We pay for the insurance, we pay for bank loans
We pay for costumes, we pay for the cell phones
We pay for the generator, we pay for sound and lights
Whatever remains, is for government babus' bribes

That's why
No *tamasha* show this season
Says the veteran *tamasgir* to me

Chirimiri economics (the economics of trivial / small bribes) it makes no sense
State subsidies are fucking nonsense
There can be no co-operative theatre movement
When we are being crushed by our own government

That's why
There will be no *tamasha* show this season
Says the veteran *tamasgir* to me

So how do the *tamasgirs* perform in Maharashtra? Beg, borrow, steal.

And if they belong to the Phule–Ambedkarite–Marxist movement, then they rebel...

SAMBHAJI BHAGAT'S STRATEGY OF SURVIVAL

Last year, Shahir Sambhaji Bhagat was felicitated at the Marathi International Film & Theatre Awards (MIFTA) in Singapore, for the music-design of his play *Shivaji Underground in Bhimnagar Mohalla*. A crowd sits in a circle. Theatrewallahs, trade unionists, scribes, socialists, Dalit Panthers and the Vidrohi cadre, and tomorrow's *shahirs*.

Sambhaji says, "We are the children of our age, and we inhabit a diminished space. Our genes have a past and a caste. Ambedkarites have been labelled as today's bad boys in Maharashtra. All that we say or do is under surveillance."

Every show he performs, be it in the slums of Mankhurd or Kurla, or on the manicured lawns of the Tata Institute of Social Sciences (TISS), he summons the god of humour and belts out a *powada*. The members of the motley audience sing along. The words of the ballad reverberate. It is about political oppression expressed through folk harmonies.

Years ago, I met another legend: the late Shahir Atmaram Patil. His poetry, songs and *powada*s were socialistic and secular.

Shahir Atmaram had said, *"Jo abhyas nahi karega, usko kya pata hoga?"* (If you don't study, you will become a nothing), referring to the political misappropriation of Shivaji by right-wing parties in Maharashtra.

I asked: "Why did this happen? Why didn't we prevent it?"

Shahir Atmaram smiled: "Shivaji ensures votes. Art doesn't."

Sambhaji follows this tradition of the *shahir*s (people's poets from the *tamasha* lexicon) in Maharashtra. He says, "After every war, someone has to tidy up. Things won't pick themselves up, after all."

Which is how his play *Shivaji Underground in Bhimnagar Mohalla* came into being.

AMBEDKAR'S MANTRA: EDUCATE, ORGANISE, AGITATE

It's been an arduous 50-odd years on this planet for Sambhaji. From a small town near Panchgani, the son of a gifted cobbler, he gravitated to the local RSS outlet for his initial schooling. Only when he reached Mumbai for further education did he realise he had been "indoctrinated". His comrades in arms at Sidhartha Hostel ensured a change in ideology. He de-programmed his system. He was asked to read Ambedkar and Marx in English. He did so. A major achievement for a hinterland boy, who could barely formulate a phrase in Marathi.

Since then, his life has entailed performances in the slums of Maharashtra for huge audiences. There was a stint in Nagpur jail in the mid-'80s for being a Naxalite. These days, he teaches in a school. When he is not teaching, he protests. He lends his voice for Sudhir Dhawale of the Vidrohi Sanghatana or for Kabir Kala Manch. Every time I watch him perform, I realise it is a tad difficult to simplify his body of work into glib phrases. When asked how and why he raises these uncomfortable questions about our times in his songs, he says, "I'm not for sale, that's why."

But it's not so simple. His performances are cock-a-snook against the cultural Stalinists, who have carefully choreographed the notion of what art is in this country. Sambhaji does not fit into the official paradigm. For one, he is a rebel. The other thing is, he is also a political soothsayer. When he sings his all-time favourite, "*Inko dhyaan se dekho re bhai / Inki soorat ko pehchano re bhai*" (Look at them carefully, brother / And recognise their real face, brother), you wonder why we were not paying heed. He seems to have anticipated our political problems quite eloquently.

Sambhaji believes, "Power grows out of music. People respond to the words in a song. That's why we need to take words to people. Too many big egos have ruined the movement. It's important to re-organise." This is what Sambhaji is seeking to do, as he concludes with Babasaheb's words, "Educate, agitate and organise."

THE TRADITION OF AMAR SHEIKH AND ANNABHAU SATHE

Sambhaji Bhagat deploys a "duff" for most of the protests and performs in *basti*s (slums) and *maidan*s (open squares) across the State. During these performances, he highlights caste discrimination. For me, he is Bob Dylan, Eminem, Gramsci, Noam Chomsky and Vivek Chibber, all rolled into one. His performances make the politics of Phule, Ambedkar and Marx crystal-clear and accessible to everyone.

He re-invented *lok shahiri* (poetry of the common people) in the tradition of Amar Sheikh and Annabhau Sathe, and became one of the gems of Indian theatre.

To understand his role, one must examine his work with the Avahan Natya Manch in the 1980s. Two things happened. One: the group included protest songs from Bhagat and Shahir Vilas Gohre in their street plays. Two: the presence of the duo, Bhagat and Gohre, meant the staging became less Brechtian and Eurocentric in its structure.

The earthiness and Indian-ness translated into plays like *Nandi Baill*, which is about the tradition of villagers questioning a bullock. So there are questions like: "Will it rain this year?" or "Will my wife return to me?" The bullock nods "yes" or "no", depending on how its handler nudges it. In other words, the bullock is manipulated by the handler. In Avahan's *Nandi Baill*, the bullock became a metaphor of Indian democracy, and how the people are brainwashed, through the bullock, by its handler.

Likewise, there was *Matdanachi Jatra,* which was a popular folk play about a child who is born on August 15th, 1947, and becomes sick. This child is examined by the crores of gods and goddesses (equal to leaders of the political parties). Will the 35-year-old child called Freedom (India was 35 in 1983) improve? Or will Freedom end up casting votes in an election booth under the diktat of the gods and goddesses?

Both plays had innumerable stagings and enjoyed cult following in the interior of Maharashtra.

In the 1980s, Shahir Bhagat raised his voice, as he continues to do so now, especially when all forms of cultural resistance have been neutralised.

In addition to singing and messaging, Shahir Sambhaji Bhagat has mentored groups like Kabir Kala Manch and Deshbhakti Yuva Manch in "the art of composing songs and a few performance tricks". These could be about social evils or promoting inter-caste marriage or anti-superstition. But above all it's about educating, agitating and organising.

KKM AND DESHBHAKTI YUVA MANCH

Educate, agitate and organise has been the strategy of groups like Kabir Kala Manch in Pune and Deshbhakti Yuva Manch in Nagpur.

I heard about DYM from Arun Ferreira, a schoolmate from St. Stanislaus in Bandra.

"It was an unusual cultural group," said Arun Ferreira, who was arrested in Dikshabhoomi in Nagpur in 2007. "After all, not often do you come across a group that works among the grassroots, putting up an act around the Theory of Relativity." One of the reasons Ferreira was arrested was his "so-called association" to the Chandrapur-based Deshbhakti Yuva Manch.

In Sewri jail, before a court session, two of the members, Anuradha Sonule and Mayuri Bhagat, talked about their work in Chandrapur, where they have staged plays in colleges and universities, including a play on Einstein during the 100 years of celebration, and how Einstein's relativity theory was the focus of one of their campaigns. In addition, the group staged anti-superstition drives, sang songs, and mobilised audiences.

The group emerged out of a Marathi daily's attempts to expand its base by supporting college and youth bands in 2002. The members of the group decided they wanted to do more than sing and dance and entertain. They charted a radical course, initiating and sustaining campaigns, mainly street theatre.

By 2005, Deshbhakti Yuva Manch had grown in stature, and had run campaigns on the birth centenary of Bhagat Singh, among other things. Their plays were political, stringing together Ambedkarite and leftist strands.

In fact, in 2007, they organised a 5,000-strong rally in Chandrapur.

There were claims that the group had enlisted over 15,000 members.

This was when the State swung into action.

In January 2008, nine members of Deshbhakti Yuva Manch were arrested for their alleged involvement in offences punishable under Sections 10, 13, 18 and 39(1) of the Unlawful Activities (Prevention) Act (UAPA), 1967, which deal with membership of an unlawful association, membership of a terrorist organisation / gang, and sympathies for a terrorist organisation / gang. They were also charged with sedition (Section 124A), criminal conspiracy (Section 120B), cheating (Section 420), forgery (Section 465), and possessing unlicensed arms.

In February 2010, Bandu Meshram, who was on the radar of the Nagpur police, was "arrested"—he was presented as "Bhanu", an absconding accused in the Deshbhakti Yuva Manch. Following his arrest, Bandu was tortured for over two weeks—he was stripped and beaten up and given electric shocks to his genitals.

According to a State report, "Bandu was associated with the Mumbai-based group called Republican Panther Jati Antachi Chalwal (RP) founded by Sudhir Dhawale, who remains in jail on charges of being a Maoist".

WHO IS SUDHIR DHAWALE?

In 2011, the Gondia police arrested Sudhir Dhawale, editor of *Vidrohi* magazine and freelance journalist based in Mumbai, on charges of waging war against the State. He was booked under the Unlawful Activities (Prevention) Act. Dhawale had been a speaker at the Youth Ambedkari Literature Festival.

The Sub-Divisional Police Officer of Devri in Gondia district, Shashikant Borate, confirmed the arrest. "We arrested him today [Monday] at 9.30 a.m.

from Wardha. He has been booked under Section 121-A of the Indian Penal Code read with sub-sections 17, 20 and 39, and under the UAPA."

The charge sheet against Dhawale acknowledges his work as a cultural activist, but makes that the grounds for his prosecution. Among other things, the charge sheet (English translation) states:

> Sudhir Pralhad Dhavale participated in the movement on students' problems along with activists of the Vidyarthi Pragati Sangathana, Anil Borkar, Sanjay Fulzele, in 1987. He worked for propaganda and spreading of the thoughts of the CPI (Maoist) through Aavhan Natya Manch. He participated in the party programme together with Anuradha Gandhi and Kobad Gandhi, Milind Teltumbade, Vernon Gonsalves, Advocate Susan Abraham and other members of the CPI (Maoist). He has written against the POTA, UAPA Acts.
>
> On January 3rd, 2011, the person of the accused was searched when a letter addressed to the Hon. Chief Minister stating "Free Dr. Binayak Sen" was found (Dr. Sen has been convicted of Naxal Crime in Chattisgarh). The accused has propagated that the action taken against Dr. Binayak Sen was false and has made propaganda against the order of the Court and thus he seems to have committed contempt of court.
>
> On January 3rd, 2011, the house of the accused was searched and copies of papers pertaining to charge sheets and other investigation papers relating to CR No. 174/2006 (The case of the burning railway engine) of Saleksa Police were seized. The accused persons in the said crime are secretary of the CPI (Maoist) Vishnu alias Sridhar Shrinivasan, Vikram alias Vernon Gonsalves, Sanjay Chaoudhary alias Arun Thomas Pereira, Subhash alias Vijay alias Ayatu Babulal Ursa, and Mahesh alias Murali alias Ashok Satya Reddi.
>
> The accused has written and published inflammatory books, such as *Introduction of Naxal Revolution*; *Charu Majumdar—Heroes of Indian Revolution*; *Operation Hunt Konasathi*; *Maovadyaviruddha Yuddha Konasathi Kashasathi* (The Battle of the Maoists—For Whom and for What?); *etc.* He has supported the philosophy of the CPI (Maoist) and the Naxal movement in these books.
>
> The accused has made false propaganda that the legal system, executive system and judicial system created by the Constitution

in democratic India is the associate of plunderers. Their objective is also evident: to overthrow this system. The accused has called the Government a terrorist and also committed contempt of court by objecting to the sacred work of delivery of justice by the judicial system.

In the book written by the accused, *Maovadyanche Yuddha Konasathi Kashasathi*, the "dedication" reads: "To her who has led the movement on both fronts of pen and gun in the Naxalbari stream of thought and in the freedom struggle of Dalits and toilers, to the revolutionary memories of dear comrade Anuradha Gandhi". The Anuradha Gandhi mentioned in the book was a member of the CPI (Maoist).

From the accused, invitation cards to a press conference convened by the accused have been seized. The press conference was against the action taken by the ATS Mumbai. The FIR copy of the crime No. 10/2007, ATS Mumbai under Section 120(B), 120(A), IPC, with Section 3, 25 of Indian Arms Act with Section 9, 10, 13, 16, 18, 20, 23 of Unlawful Activities (Prevention) Act has been seized. In this crime, the accused person is Shridhar Shrinivasan, the Secretary of the CPI (Maoist). Efforts are made to bring pressure on the police and the judicial system through a press conference and by objecting to the action taken by the ATS Mumbai.

A computer CPU and articles have been seized.

The arrested accused Sudhir was present for 12 days at the secret session held in October, 2006 at Mumbai, Christian Sanatorium, Virar, Mumbai. Accused Sudhir had given guidance in the Naxal secret session about the party constitution, party programme, political proposals, war tactics, work tactics, funds and finance subjects. He is a Naxalite Area Commander who wears plainclothes and lives in the city doing Naxal work.

The charge sheet concludes:

The accused Sudhir Dhavale worked for propaganda and spreading of the CPI (Maoist) by staying at Mumbai. He worked to train the members of the organisation in organisational, political, party constitution, party programme subjects by holding secret meetings of the Maharashtra State Committee which he guided, remaining present during the meetings of the banned organisation CPI (Maoist).

> By writing books and literature about Naxalism, he has made inflammatory writings for antagonising the people against the legislative system, executive and judicial systems and Government and waged war against the Indian Government in collusion. Also, he did the work of spreading and propagating the thoughts of the said organisation through party programmes, meetings of Aavhan Natya Manch. He has written against the POTA, UAPA laws.

Dhawale's wife said the arrest and the raid were unexpected. "They [the police] have been picking up any book or magazine red in colour because they want to prove a connection to Naxalism. They have taken so many books on Marx, Lenin."

THREE LESSONS FOR ME

There are three key points I understand from all of this...

One. In most of the above cases, policemen are shown as the complainant, thereby throwing into doubt the veracity of the case.

Two. Also, most cases of this nature are lodged in Gadchiroli, even though the accused might be based in Mumbai. For instance, although Sudhir Dhawale was based in Mumbai, he was arrested in Wardha and the case was lodged in that district. In my view, this is a ploy on the part of the State to avoid publicity and media glare. The mantra is: Picked up in Mumbai, encountered in Bihar. Dhawale is not the only example of this. Other examples include: Saibaba, Prashat Rahi and Hem Mishra.

Three. And finally when State action against a cultural group becomes total and complete, it compels members to go underground. For instance, in the Saibaba case, like the Binayak Sen case, the accusation is "a letter for the Maoist". Does such an act constitute an offence? Even if the Maoist leadership is criminalised as determined by the State, does the act of giving a letter or communicating with an alleged criminal constitute a crime?

So...

HOW DOES ONE COUNTER ALL THIS?

Theatre artistes like me have tried to do this in three ways:

One. As part of the KKM Defence Committee, one has (in a very limited manner—which is the other thing, we need better defence committees in India) made an attempt to create awareness through forums, including the present one, and ensure legal redress and funding for members of the group. Be it: to produce CDs of their songs or to organise press conferences or performances of their shows.

Two. To continue to write plays. In 2010, I was tired of signing petitions and attending court hearings and rallies. So I tried to do what I think I know best. I wrote a play called *Comrade Kumbhakarna* in the naïve hope that it would gain freedom for Arun Ferreira, Shridhar Srinivasan, Vernon Gonsalves and K.D. Rao.

Through a cruel twist of irony (and I love theatre because I love ironies), the NSD produced and staged this play, which was directed by Mohit Takalkar. It did around 50 shows in Hindi, which meant this message could reach out.

There is a scene in the play. The B-grade actor who plays Kumbhakarna in a B-grade *nautanki* (a form of folk opera) is arrested by the equivalent of the ATS or Anti-Naxal Operations.

This is what happens on stage in *Comrade Kumbhakarna*:

> *The stage resembles an interrogation room. The bureaucrats Iyer and Nair are seated. A camera plus light is switched on to record proceedings. Kumbhakarna enters. He is chained,* etc.
>
> **Iyer:** Ah, Comrade Kumbhakarna, you're here. For your knowledge, this trial is being conducted in a PWD guest house. Please, please do be seated.
>
> **Nair:** Welcome. Hope your stay has been comfortable? Food supply? Clean water? Medicine?
>
> **Iyer:** Any complaints?
>
> *No response from Kumbhakarna.*
>
> **Nair:** Good. This is your FIR. Will you sign the NOC document?
>
> *No response from Kumbhakarna.*
>
> **Iyer:** Ah well *(polite laugh)*. Dear Comrade Kumbhakarnaji, would you like to say hello to our camera which is recording this interview?
>
> *Emphatic shaking of head from Kumbhakarna.*

Nair: Oh, just as well... As you know, you were arrested on a Sunday. In the fish market. With a dangerous anti-national subversive document. It contains the formulae of how to build a bomb.

Kumbhakarna: Er... it is my grocery shopping list.

Iyer: Arre-Arre. Comrade Kumbhakarna... please cease your interruptions.

Kumbhakarna is forced to have a pill.

Nair: Comrade Kumbhakarna—just to remind you—we have 18 cases against you under 120(B), 121(A), 124(A), 153 A& B of the IPC, and sec 38, 39 and 40 of the UAPA, 2004... Please note: You will not receive bail for three years on charges of sedition, waging war against the State, conspiracy and supporting a banned Asura organisation.

The pill takes an effect on Kumbhakarna.

Iyer: Ssssh. Look he has fallen asleep. In fact, he is snoring.

Nair: He truly and positively is. This is a complete and unmitigated disaster.

END

There is a slice of life in the above scene.

I stole it from the life of Vernon Gonsalves on August 19th, 2007. Vernon was arrested outside his home on a Sunday morning in 2007, in the heart of Mumbai in Mahakali Caves, Andheri East. The said "grocery list" was the weapon the State used as evidence against him. Nineteen charges were pressed. This included being a top Naxalite leader and harbouring explosives and such-like.

Three. The third way is: celebrate the GOOD NEWS.

Today, after six years in prison (2007 to 2013), Vernon Gonsalves has been released. So have Arun Ferreira, Shridhar Srinivasan and K.D. Rao.

Long live optimism.

Naïveness zindabad.

I met Vernon Gonsalves post his release with a gift of Swedish crime thrillers.

This is what he said:

> The ruling classes and media have made the term "Naxalite" so synonymous with terrorist that anyone would be wary of admitting to be a Naxalite. But a Naxalite is in no way a terrorist. A Naxalite is one who upholds the 1967 struggle of the tribal peasants of Naxalbari village of West Bengal as showing the path for the struggles of the people of our country, and it is in that sense I am a Naxalite. Needless to say, I am no terrorist and stand strongly opposed to terrorism.

Vernon adds:

> I do not think that the Maharashtra ATS was particularly interested in my earlier trade union work in Vidarbha. They were, at the most, interested in doing some arrests to show some activity on their part with regards to Naxalism. They created a false case by fabricating an FIR and fake *panchnama* (documentation of an arrest by witnesses) with their own stock *panch* witnesses. The Anti-Naxal Operations (ANO) then got me implicated in seventeen further cases, involving serious offences like murder. They well knew I had nothing to do with these cases and that I had not even been mentioned in the FIRs or in any of the case papers prior to my arrest. This is the way these agencies function.

BAD BRUTALITY VS. GOOD VIOLENCE

The show has become chaotic. The performances seem to make no head or tail to "we, the people".

With Kabir Kala Manch's frequent allusions to democracy's failures, oppression, and domination of one caste over the other, it was on the State's radar. When Sheetal Sathe sang about how Ambedkar said if the Constitution did not give people justice—political, social and economic—his people should overthrow it, the State started to act. It's bad brutality vs. good violence justice—that's the explanation from the civil rights camp.

The State counter-argues, based on a confessional statement under section 164 of the criminal procedure code, that members of the Kabir Kala Manch had an affair with the Naxalite ideology of the CPI (Maoist), who indoctrinated them. The charge: training camps in Pune's Khed *taluka* (administrative section), lecturing in support of imprisoned Angela Sontakke and others, rubbing shoulders with revolutionaries and visiting campuses and *bastis* (slums) with "a message in the service of a cause".

When Kabir Kala Manch members meet us at Sewri Court, their literary inspiration is still not exhausted.

Deepak Dengle hands me a poem, *Inquilab Chahiye*. In the poem, he seeks in art a fulfilment that had eluded him in life. The poem is in Hindi and has a rudimentary rhythm. He sings the first *mukhda* (introductory section):

Ek mutthi baandho reh baandho
Ek mutthi baandho re doston
Bas ek mukka chahiye
Aur ek dhakka chahiye
Inquilab chaiye doston
Inquilab

(Clench your hand into a fist, Clench it
Clench it tight into a fist
Just one punch is enough
Just one push is enough
Friends, we need a revolution
Revolution)

The police battalion gathers around Dengle to eavesdrop. They are bemused.

Meanwhile, suspected women Maoist sympathisers lodged in Mumbai District Women's Prison in Byculla are brought to the Sessions Court at Sewri by a posse of policemen and policewomen. These are "the dangerous Maoist sympathisers": Angela Sontakke, Sushma Ramteke, Anuradha Sonule, Mayuri Bhagat, as well as 19-year-old Jyoti Chorghe.

They had been arrested in Pune by the anti-terrorism squad (ATS) under the Unlawful Activities (Prevention) Act, 1967.

And in this way, the show goes on.

It is not all doom and gloom; there is a glimmer of hope…

In true Bollywood fashion we CUT TO…

THE HIGH COURT OF JUDICATURE AT BOMBAY... CRIMINAL APPELLATE JURISDICTION

It is time to study the *Criminal Bail Application*. And see how Abhay Mahadeo Thipsay (brother of chess champ, Praveen Thipsay) pronounced a very progressive judgement in two cases of KKM members.

One: Jyoti Babasaheb Chorge and Sushma Ramtekke... Applicants versus State of Maharashtra... Respondent (delivered on October 12th, 2012)

And the second: Dhawala Deepak Dengle and others... Applicants versus State of Maharashtra ... (Delivered on January 31st, 2013)

The first judgement, a 26-page document, says many important things about India and democracy. The key points are:

> That the possession of certain literature having a particular social or political philosophy would amount to an offence, though such literature is not expressly or specifically banned under any provision of law, is a shocking proposition in a democratic country like ours. A feeble attempt to put forth such a proposition was made by the Learned Special Public Prosecutor (representing the State) in the oral arguments.
>
> Such a proposition runs counter to the freedoms and rights guaranteed by Article 19 of the Constitution. In this regard, a reference may also be made to a decision of the Gujarat High Court, on which reliance has been placed by Shri Mihir Desai. (Criminal Miscellaneous Application Nos. 12435 to 12437 and other connected applications, decided on 18.11.2010).
>
> The applicants therein had been alleged to be in contact with a person involved in the Naxal movement and serious charges of offences punishable under Sections 121A, 124A, 153A, 120B, *etc.*, of the IPC were levelled against them along with offences punishable under Sections 38, 39 and 40 of the UAP Act (as it stood then).
>
> While releasing the applicants on bail, the High Court observed that the seizure of the so-called incriminating material, by itself, cannot show participation in an activity prohibited by law. It was held that mere possession of such literature, without actual execution of the ideas contained therein, would not amount to any offence.

The judgement continues...

The applicants are young persons. The applicant Jyoti is of 19 years and the applicant Sushma is of 26 years. They are in custody since April 2011. It appears that they come from a poor family. A number of persons are influenced, and get attracted towards the Maoist philosophy because of the oppression of the weaker section which they might have experienced in the social set-up. The applicants also, like a number of such persons, might have been influenced and impressed by the Maoist philosophy.

It has been recognised even by the committees appointed by the government to study the problem of Naxalites that it is the social, political, economic and cultural discrimination faced by the poor that is throwing a large number of discontented people towards the Maoists. It is impossible to hold that all such persons are to be treated as members of a terrorist organisation, or that they are liable to be punished for having some faith in such philosophy, or for having sympathy for those who propagate such philosophy.

It is in this context, that the concept of active membership and passive membership has been judicially evolved.

In the result, the following order is passed: The applications are allowed.

Operative Order in Bail Application No.1020 of 2012: The applicant (for Jyoti Babasaheb Chorge of Kabir Kala Manch) is ordered to be released on bail in the sum of Rs 30,000, with one surety in like amount, or two sureties in the sum of Rs 15,000 each, on the condition that she shall report to Dhankavdi Police Station, Pune, on every Sunday, till the disposal of the case against her.

Likewise, the Operative Order in Bail Application No. 1066 of 2012: The applicant (for Sushma Hemant Ramtekke of Kabir Kala Manch) is ordered to be released on bail in the sum of Rs 30,000, with one surety in like amount, or two sureties in the sum of Rs 15,000 each, on the condition that she shall report to Ajni Police Station, Nagpur City, on every Sunday, till the disposal of the case against her.

Signed
(ABHAY M. THIPSAY, J)

Meanwhile, fantasy and fact cross paths. What is this beast called free speech? Should the State be in a position to ban all political activity it is uncomfortable with from these lands? Are these futile pontifications?

After the new government in Delhi was constituted, the Union Home Minister meets all the DGPs. A statement by the DGP from the state I belong to states he will target all so-called intellectuals who support the Maoist cause. It's literally thumbing one's nose at Thipsay's judgement.

IS THIS THE END, MY FRIENDS...

Not really... Anuradha Sonule gets her bail executed after one year, due to innumerable rules and entanglements.

Meanwhile, Sudhir Dhawale is acquitted. In a bit of Dario Fo-style satire, the State's Home Minister in a media stunt threatens to resign. After the acquittal, he backtracks. It has been reported that police officers tried to prejudice the verdict with a polite visit to the court premises on the previous day.

The police continue to visit the *bastis* and fish markets where Deepak Dengle, Sidharth Bhosale and others are working or staying in Pune. Meanwhile, bail has been granted to Sheetal Sathe. But bail applications are pending for Sachin, Sagar and Ramesh, where the magistrate has been transferred, yet again.

Jai Rashtra.

Jai Maha-Rashtra.

The Spatial Dimensions of Property: Notes from Lamington Road in Mumbai

Prasad Shetty & Rupali Gupte

With its explosive growth and extremely diverse population, Mumbai is something of a "special case", as T.W. Geraghty puts it later in this book. Here, Prasad Shetty and Rupali Gupte analyse the "unique urbanity" of this remarkable city, focusing on a single street.

Shetty and Gupte are themselves urbanists based in Mumbai. They trained as architects and specialise in urban management and urban design respectively. They are co-founders of the urban research collective CRIT (crit.in) and of the School of Environment and Architecture (sea.edu.in).

Consider the following description:

> The street is narrow with two-storeyed buildings on either side that have balconies on the upper floors and arcades on the ground. They almost touch each other sideways, forming a continuous wall along the street embellished with uninterrupted balconies and arcades on the ground floor. Small and large shops on the ground floor of the buildings open into the arcades. The street is more than a mile long and connects two major roads of the city. The shops are popular and provide enough opportunities to fulfil all kinds of desires. While it remains busy the entire day, the evenings are significant, when the bright colourful signboards of the shops switch on. Every evening on this street appears to be a carnival.

In this description, the street is an "urban space". It being more than a mile long, having shop fronts on either sides, its narrowness, two-storeyed height, with continuous strips of balconies, uninterrupted arcades, bright and colourful signboards, large numbers of people walking, *etc.*, are the "distinguishable physicalities" of the urban space, or the "urban form". All urban spaces have distinct urban form. The street described above is evidently different from a highway or a city artery. Similarly, different neighbourhoods in the city will have their own distinct urban forms—some neighbourhoods have narrow streets and buildings touching the street; some have wide streets where the edges of the street have sidewalks, which in turn are edged with high boundary walls enclosing buildings; some are made of tall commercial buildings; some are predominantly residential high rises, and so on. Different qualities get attributed to different urban spaces based on form. For example, an incrementally developed neighbourhood, where people have built their own houses, could appear dense and "slum"-like. On the other hand, a neighbourhood that is developed on a grid plan with wide roads and rectangular plots would appear completely different. Attributes such as organised, informal, clean, dirty, safe, unsafe, congested, sparse, ordered, *etc.*, are formed about urban space. The urban form also produces an urban life. In the above description, the street is a place of enterprise, it fulfils desires; it is like a carnival, *etc.*

For our present purposes, "property" is specifically "real-property"—land, buildings, urban space, real-estate, fixtures on land, *etc.* Real property is produced through "claims" of people. In urban India, the claims over land are complex and can be of various kinds. There may be many parties making different claims over a single piece of land—all coexisting and simultaneous. For example, a person may have obtained a piece of land from the State on lease and then rented it to a company, which has built houses and shops over it. Hence, all parties involved have various kinds of simultaneous coexisting claims that are not necessarily contradictory to each other. The overlap of customary holding of land with the "*one land–one party*" titling system brings about other kinds of complexities. For instance, in many parts of pre-colonial India, lands were claimed jointly by several people—feudal lords, tillers, family members, community members, *etc.* In many places, such joint claims continued after Independence. However, the modern systems of land transactions and development that were put in place by the government were compatible with the "one land–one party" titling system. Lands with joint claims became extremely difficult to transact or develop. Claims also exist by prolonged occupation of property. For example, a person living in a place for more than a certain number of years cannot be evicted in many parts of India. Property in urban areas gets formed through all kinds of claims—claims of a title holder, a tenant, a sub-tenant, a part-holder of title, an occupant of premises for several years, and so on.

We shall discuss the relationship between urban form and urban property through the case of a neighbourhood in Mumbai. The neighbourhood is an electronics cluster along a street called *Lamington Road*.

1 THE STREET

Like many other streets in Mumbai, Lamington Road displays some amount of clarity during the early hours of the day when the shops are still shut. If one walks the street during this time, three distinct parts of the street are identifiable—a carriageway in the centre with four car lanes; two reasonably wide walkways along the edges of the carriageway; and a line of buildings along the edges of the walkways. The buildings almost touch each other, forming a continuous boundary to the street, and have shops on the ground floor. The traffic is very thin during the early hours and there is an occasional car parked along the edge of the carriageway. The walkway has several kinds of installations on its edge along the carriageway. Usually, these are large wooden boxes or rag-tag tables made of make-shift wooden pieces. These are the *sidewalk-shops* which start business around ten o'clock in the morning. Many wooden pieces are attached to these boxes and tables to provide necessary extensions for shading the shop or increasing storage. In some cases, the tables and boxes have things kept on them. These things are neatly covered with thick plastic sheets and secured to the boxes and tables with tightly-tied ropes. It is difficult to make out what these things could be as only a vague form is seen covered in plastic. In many cases, the doors of the boxes are locked with large padlocks.

Though the sidewalk-shops are secured with ropes and locks, they look extremely vulnerable to burglars operating during the night. A few homeless men sleep on the sidewalks during the night. Some of them are employed by the sidewalk-shopkeepers to guard their shops and wares. The shops along the other side of the sidewalk, in the buildings, seem to be of all sizes—their shutters measure anywhere between a metre to about six metres. One can figure out two kinds of shops: *building-shops* that are deep and become the ground floor of the buildings, and *one-foot-shops* that are simply embedded in the walls. These one-foot shops dig themselves one foot within the wall and extend themselves one foot outside. They usually come up on the free part of the wall between two building-shops. All the shops along the buildings have metal rolling shutters covering them. A deep and thick awning generally protrudes above the shutters of each building-shop. The name of the shop is displayed on the front of the awning.

As the day progresses, the vehicular traffic on the carriageway increases, and some of the night-guards start sweeping the sidewalks. A few men open the shutters of the building-shops and start bringing out empty cardboard boxes and keeping them next to the doors of the shops. The cardboard boxes make customers believe they can get what they are looking for. Most of the times, when the shops do not have the requisite items with them, the shopkeeper calls a few nearby shops to get them. The customer is never left disappointed.

The sidewalk-shopkeepers also arrive and start setting up their shops. Many of the shopkeepers carry their wares with them, which are brought from the adjoining buildings. They rent spaces in the building to store their wares. Usually these spaces are within houses. The shopkeepers pay a small amount to the family occupying the house to rent a part of the house during the night. Some of the sidewalk-shopkeepers may rent the spaces within the thick awnings of the building-shops.

The one-foot-shopkeepers also open their shops. When these open, they become much larger objects. Their insides unfold into several small shelves with colourful wares, turning these benign-looking boxes into glittering, magical creatures. The street has a few other shops selling vegetables, fruits and flowers. The vendors using these shops sell most of their stock during the day time, leaving only a cadaver of the shop at night that waits to gain life again the next day with fresh stock. Sometimes, different vendors occupy the same space during different hours of the day—for example, a newspaper vendor and a flower vendor may use the same premises in shifts.

Then there is the day and night shop—when the day shop shuts, the night shop takes over its closed shutters. And at certain times of the day, even the surfaces of the parked cars become temporary shops.

Urban property in Lamington Road seems to be configured through multiple claims and does not come across as a clear entity belonging to a single person. Boundaries, that are so essential to define property, get constantly made, erased and re-made through claims of different people—homeless night occupiers, building-shopkeepers, one-foot-shopkeepers, sidewalk-shopkeepers, vegetable and fruit sellers, newspaper vendors, buyers and casual walkers.

This dynamic nature of claims and property has its impact on the urban form of the street. A visitor walking in Lamington Road has to pass through capillaries formed by the juxtaposition of various kinds of shops. It is often difficult to identify where one shop ends and another begins. All things along the edge of the street, including the visitors and shop-owners, diffuse into one another. The urban form is blurred and has a very high transactional capacity. It allows many activities to take place. In this blur, the differences set up by notions of public and private space, concepts of inside and outside and all other ideas that define spaces through clear boundaries are challenged. Urban form seems to be clearly a function of claims.

2 THE CHAWL

Lamington Road borders on the inner city areas of Mumbai. These areas acquired their intensity about two centuries ago, when they were converted from paddy fields and vegetable orchards to a marketplace. The development of a port in Mumbai along the eastern edge of the city in the 1700s attracted large numbers of traders and other trade workers. The farmers of Mumbai found it more profitable to convert their large houses and fields into rented accommodation for traders than to continue with farming. They also started developing multi-storeyed buildings with tiny rooms for rent. These were called "chawls". Some traders actually bought land from farmers to build chawls.

The chawls usually had shops and offices on the ground floors and residential units on the higher floors. The process of converting agricultural lands into rented built-form happened slowly over time—initially, only small and non-fertile parts were used, but later, as demand for housing and shops increased, more and more land was converted. By the early 1900s, this part of the city was entirely turned into a dense place for trading and living.

Several religious, educational, community and artistic institutions also developed to provide a cultural support to the place. It produced an urbanity like a cauldron, where activities of working, recreating, chatting, praying, cooking, sleeping, gathering, *etc.*, mixed with each other. The chawl stood as a unit of such a cauldron and shaped the space and form of this urbanity.

A typical chawl consists of small one- or two-room tenements strung along a long corridor. Toilets are usually outside at the end of the corridor. A medium-sized chawl is ground-floor plus two upper storeys, and has around 70-100 tenements. Each tenement is about 10-15 square metres in size and normally has about 5-8 persons living in it. Chawls usually have an internal courtyard, which becomes an important community space for the inhabitants.

Initially, a group of male friends lived in each tenement of the chawl, but later as the place became more hospitable and the opportunities increased, the traders and others brought their families to live in the chawls.

After the 1850s, cotton textile mills appeared in the northern parts, outside the inner-city areas. People, largely men, from all over the country came to Mumbai to work in these mills. Along with the mills, chawls were developed as housing for the mill workers. Here again, usually a group of 5 to 8 men would share a tenement and its rent. Before the chawls, the pastoral communities of Mumbai either lived in large independent agrarian houses or in small, shack-like dwellings within tightly-packed hamlets. With the growth of trade and industries in the city, the chawl house had become the urban house-type of Mumbai.

Most of the migrant workers usually lived in the city for around eight to nine months and went back to their villages and families during the rainy season to farm. For these migrants, the sense of property back in the village was different from what it was in Mumbai. The place they considered home was in the village, where they had their families. The idea of "permanence" was associated with the village house. The chawl house on the other hand was simply a place to sleep. Here in the city, their idea of property was feeble—it was a small nebulous sleeping place, which was not permanent. Through the chawl, Mumbai had produced a diffused notion of a house and property.

After India's partition in 1947, large numbers of people came to India from across the new border. Because large cities could offer opportunities, they became attractive destinations for these people. As these cities experienced an overnight explosion in their population, the demand for housing increased rapidly. With the increased demand, the house rents also spiralled. The chawl-owners of Mumbai increased the rents significantly and evicted older tenants who were unable to pay them. Responding to this, the government enacted the Rent Control Act of 1948.

This Act did two things: first, it froze the rents at 1940 rates and, second, it prohibited the eviction of tenants. As tenants could no longer be thrown out of a chawl tenement, they acquired a new sense of property: the urban house was no longer just a sleeping place, but a permanent home. Friends living together in the chawl tenement split up and each would try to obtain his own independent tenement. With this new sense of property, the mill workers got their families into the city. The chawl community became consolidated, and life changed in the chawl.

The multiple claims created through the "non-eviction" policy made the buying and selling of property or change of tenancy difficult, as neither the landlord nor the tenant could make any property transactions without each other's permission. To deal with this deadlock, the practice of *Pagadi* came into existence, in which the revenue from the transactions on property was shared between the landlord and the tenant. Though this did not have a legal basis for a long time, thousands of properties were transacted through this practice.

Some of the tenants furthermore rented out a part of their tenement to a sub-tenant. The Rent Control Act also applied to such sub-tenants, and over time, they too became part of the chawl. There were sub-tenants occupying spaces under staircases, lofts, walls, and any other spaces in the chawl. With every inch of it being claimed, occupied and protected, the form of the chawl started to become blurred.

All clear spaces became encrusted with additions, and extensions erupted from everywhere. Old furniture was left in common spaces to be used by everyone. Over time, people forgot whom such loose furniture belonged to. It became part of the chawl's corroded form. Some chawls became denser than the densest slums. But everything in the chawl was protected and perfectly legal.

Usually, the long tenements in a chawl have doors on both sides, which open onto corridors that are also on both sides—the front and the rear. As the houses are small and the occupants are many, the doors are kept open throughout the day. People freely pass through each other's tenements and most of the day gets spent in corridors and the courtyard.

It is as though the entire chawl were one large continuous space, with small pockets of intensities that close themselves into small rooms during the night. The house happens during the night, with the doors shutting. A series of folding furniture—folding tables, doors that double up as cupboards, chairs that open up into beds, *etc.*, were devised to multiply space inside the tenements when required.

The form of the chawl blurred personal boundaries, producing a continuous urban space with pockets of intensities that could be identified as houses or shops. It is this blurred and continuous urban form that lends a certain logic to Mumbai—here people associate a sense of permanence and property to an unbounded space. Such a blurred space enhances transactions, provides safety, optimises resources, affords a very high occupancy and produces a unique urbanity.

3 THE APARTMENT

In the past five decades, Lamington Road has been transformed from a street popular for automobile spare-parts and accessories in the '50s and '60s, to a sound and electronics cluster in the '70s and '80s, to a computer assembly and repair node in the 1990s and early 2000s, to a market that sells branded computers, mobile phones, new media hardware, surveillance devices, specialised sound systems, and so on. The people who frequent Lamington Road have changed accordingly—from automobile mechanics, to electronic technicians, computer assemblers, to new media specialists. Branded goods came with their own logic. The informal entrepreneurship of small repair had given way to corporate call-centre-centric service centres. Of course, the service centres themselves remained largely informal and were handled primarily by contract labour that had fallen out of the earlier repair economy.

By the 1990s, there was not much land in Mumbai left for new construction. This constrained the supply of real-estate, pushing the prices even higher. With real-estate prices hitting the sky, property developers became extremely aggressive in creating new real-estate. On the other hand, some of the chawls had started deteriorating on account of intense usage. Since the 1960s, there have been instances of old chawls falling. The government had also set up a "Repairs Board" to repair such old chawls. But due to the enormity of scale and lack of capacity, the Repairs Board was not very successful in maintaining the chawls. The dilapidation of the chawls produced enough opportunity for aggressive developers to create new real-estate.

This was done by demolishing the chawls and building skyscrapers in their place. The government policy allowed and encouraged such "redevelopment" projects. For the government, redevelopments did two things: first, they created new housing stock for people living in old dilapidated chawls and, second, they also produced new real-estate for the city. The redevelopment policy was populist in its orientation and promised a free house of a minimum standard on freehold basis to all existing tenants of the chawl. The money for building such houses to rehabilitate all the tenants came from new real estate that was to be developed on the same plot and sold in the open market. Most of the central areas of Mumbai, including Lamington Road, now have a number of such redeveloped buildings.

The new rehabilitation houses are, however, completely different from the old chawl houses. They are small, self-contained apartments, with each apartment having a little living room, a tiny kitchen, a bathroom and a toilet. All of this is fitted into a minimum of 25 square metres of floor area. The living room is sometimes further divided into two smaller rooms, one of which is then called a bedroom. This subdivision generally creates dingy corridors inside the houses. There are usually no common corridors like those in the chawls. And unlike those in the chawls, these corridors never get used as community spaces. Moreover, the doors of the houses usually remain closed throughout the day.

The apartment as a house-type came to Mumbai in the 1920s when the British government created large housing schemes for attracting the educated sections of Indian society to Mumbai. The government required educated people to run the public institutions of Mumbai. These "educated" Indians, however, were from the upper castes, who have historically indulged in extreme exploitation of lower castes. People from the lowest of the lower castes, the so-called "Untouchables", usually cleaned the toilets of the people from the upper castes. The toilets were considered dirty, and since it was Untouchables who cleaned them, they would normally be located outside the living quarters of a typical upper caste house. So when the new "apartments" of Mumbai with toilets *inside* were offered to educated upper caste families, they did not accept them. Many questions were asked: How could a toilet be inside the house? How would it be cleaned? Would the Untouchable come inside the house to clean the toilets? This would pollute the entire house, and how could such a house be purified?

The architects and engineers then came up with an innovative idea to solve this problem: they made two doors to enter such houses, one that led straight to the toilets and a second door for the rest of the house. While the lower caste toilet cleaner would use the door that led to the toilets, the occupants of the house would use the other, "pure" doorway. In the Indian Institute of Technology (IIT) in Chennai, this innovation reached new heights. There, apartments had *three* doors: one to the living quarters, one straight to the kitchen, and the third straight to the toilet. But, unlike in Mumbai, where the apartments were built by either traders or real-estate developers or the British government, in IIT Chennai these apartments were built by one of the modern institutions of the socialist-leaning, democratic, secular Republic of India!

By the 1960s, the "apartment" had hijacked the idea of a house in Mumbai and also got established as a "standard house". All other forms of houses—the chawl house, the old village house, a house in an incremental settlement, *etc.*, were considered inferior to the apartment house. Typically, in the apartment of the 1960s and 1970s, the common spaces were made very small and internal spaces were maximised. The idea of the house as the "private space" of a family was established. While the chawls and early apartments were built by landlords whose business was to make rented accommodation, the delivery system of the apartments of the 1960s, and 1970s was very different. They were built by cooperative housing societies, which would buy land from the government, borrow money from banks, appoint their architects and contractors, and build their apartments. As the money had to be borrowed, there had to be a mortgage. This mortgage was the house itself. Such a house had to have clear titles as mortgage was not possible on property with multiple claims—the bank would not know whom to run after in case of non-payment, and it would be difficult to follow-up with all the claimants. The relationship between banks and property was becoming consolidated, and this required clear titles.

In the 1980s however, the cooperative movement of Mumbai was hijacked by private developers, who formed fake cooperative societies to get land from the government. They took on the responsibility of organising funds, hiring architects and contractors, managing approvals, *etc.* The housing delivery system had changed from renting up until the 1950s to self-building in the 1960s and 1970s to buying from a developer from the 1980s on. This was very good for the banks, the investors, the contractors, the architects, the government, and so on. They now had to deal with only one agent—the developer.

The developer of the 1980s was usually a tout-like character, who would manage difficult things like getting finance, land, and approvals, through bribes and favours. The real-estate market has been good throughout, except for a couple of short spells since the 1990s, and the developers quickly grew into omnipresent agents in the housing and real-estate market. They turned themselves into large corporate houses by the end of the last century, and today exist as large companies. However, the corporatisation has only enhanced and organised their tout-like behaviour—the bribes had become larger and the favours more sophisticated. Moreover, the "developer" of today cannot be identified as a single person anchoring all activities of real-estate production—the developer is rather a constellation of investors, land assemblers, financers, lawyers, accountants, architects, liaison agents, government officers, real-estate agents, contractors, plumbers, landscape consultants, *etc.* And the configuration of this constellation changes with every new real-estate project. It appears that the real-estate sector has a large set of people who form smaller groups as and when required. Putting together a house had become a large industry—and this industry needed a clear standard commodity that could be reproduced over and over again. The modern planning rules specified such standards, and irrespective of what was happening to the city economy, whether it required shelter for migrants, or single women, or transit workers, or call-centre workers, or anyone else, only apartments were built. This mixture of rules for standardisation and investment that required clarity of tenure became the prime reason for the production of apartments.

Life changed when the apartments started replacing chawls in Lamington Road. The edges and boundaries were guarded, and their blurring was not possible. The one-foot shop, the sidewalk-shop, and the other vendors started disappearing wherever the apartments came. On the upper floors, the common corridor where most of the living happened disappeared and now people were restricted within their flats. Since titles had become extremely clear, buying and selling of property proliferated. The old community that lived in the chawl found the apartment difficult to adjust to. The apartment created its own new community.

We have argued that, first, that there is a relationship between urban property, urban form, urban space and urban life; second, that the logic of Mumbai is derived from its form, which is blurred and continuous; and, third, that increasingly, there is an effort to change this form and hence change the logic of the city. Property has a spatial dimension and with every change in the idea of property, the spatial dimension changes. The multiple claims shaped the blurred street edges; the "non-eviction" enacted in the Rent Control Act created the diffused and continuous space of the chawl; and the housing delivery requirements of clear titles produced the bounded apartment. Each of these property and spatial forms produced its own distinct city life.

Three Poems

Arundhathi Subramaniam

Arundhathi Subramaniam is one of India's best-known poets. According to her Wikipedia biography, she is "a poet and writer on spirituality and culture", but she also has a very strong sense of place, as evidenced in her poems about Bombay / Mumbai, and a keen awareness of identity.

THE CITY AND I

(returning to Bombay after November 26, 2008)

This time we didn't circle each other
hackles raised,
fur bristling.

This time there was space
between us—
and we weren't competing.

Space enough and more
for the nose-digging librarian
and her stainless steel tiffin box,

for the Little Theatre peon to read me
his Marathi poems
on rainy afternoons

for the woman on the 7.10 Bhayandar slow
with green combs in her hair
to say
and say again,

He's coming to get me.
He's coming

This time
the city surged
towards me

mangy
bruised-eyed
non-vaccinated

suddenly
mine.

TO THE WELSH CRITIC WHO DOESN'T FIND ME IDENTIFIABLY INDIAN

You believe you know me,
wide-eyed Eng Lit type
from a sun-scalded colony,
reading my Keats—or is it yours—
while my country detonates
on your television screen.

You imagine you've cracked
my deepest fantasy—
oh, to be in an Edwardian vicarage,
living out my dharma
with every sip of dandelion tea
and dreams of the weekend jumble sale…

You may have a point.
I know nothing about silly mid-offs,
I stammer through my Tamil,
and I long for a nirvana
that is hermetic,
odour-free,
bottled in Switzerland,
money-back-guaranteed.

This business about language,
how much of it is mine,
how much yours,
how much from the mind,
how much from the gut,
how much is too little,
how much too much,
how much from the salon,
how much from the slum,
how I say verisimilitude,

how I say Brihadaranyaka,
how I say vaazhapazham—
it's all yours to measure,
the pathology of my breath,
the halitosis of gender,
my homogenised plosives
about as rustic
as a mouth-freshened global village.

Arbiter of identity,
remake me as you will.
Write me a new alphabet of danger,
a new patois to match
the Chola bronze of my skin.
Teach me how to come of age
in a literature you've bark-scratched
into scripture.
Smear my consonants
with cow-dung and turmeric and godhuli.
Pity me, sweating,
rancid, on the other side of the counter.
Stamp my papers,
lease me a new anxiety,
grant me a visa
to the country of my birth.
Teach me how to belong,
the way you do,
on every page of world history.

WHERE I LIVE

(for Anders who wants to know)

I live on a wedge of land
reclaimed from a tired ocean
somewhere at the edge of the universe.

Greetings from this city
of L'Oreal sunsets
and diesel afternoons,
deciduous with concrete,
botoxed with vanity.

City of septic magenta hair-clips,
of garrulous sewers and tight-lipped taps,
of '80s film tunes buzzing near the left temple,
of ranting TV soaps and monsoon melodramas.

City wracked by hope and bulimia.
City uncontained
by movie screen and epigram.
City condemned to unspool
in an eternal hysteria
of lurid nylon dream.
City where you can drop off
a swollen local
and never be noticed.
City where you're a part
of every imli-soaked bhelpuri.

City of the Mahalaxmi beggar
peering up through
a gorse-bush of splayed limbs.
City of dark alleys,

city of mistrust,
city of forsaken tube-lit rooms.

City that coats the lungs
stiffens the spine
chills the gut
with memory
City suspended between
flesh
      and mortar
                and foam leather
                                    and delirium

where it is perfectly historical
to be looking out
on a sooty handkerchief of ocean,
searching for God.

THE SHARED SPACE OF BOLLYWOOD

Jerry Pinto

Jerry Pinto is a Goan-born, Mumbai-based, prize-winning Indian writer of poetry, prose and children's fiction in English, as well as a journalist. In 2016, he was awarded the prestigious Windham-Campbell Literary Prize (administered by Yale University).

Bharat dil hai us purab ka
Jis purab ne har gyaan kiya
Diye Buddha, Mohammed aur Isaa
Geeta, Bible, Quran diya.

—Lyrics from *Purab aur Pachchim* (Manoj Kumar, 1970)

First things first. Bollywood is popular culture. Like all other popular culture, it is created largely by men and women who are seeking to get rich, who love glamour, who like the business of selling dreams. What good it does, it does by accident. But simply because it is popular, its reach is tremendous, its power rests on the dangerously shifting ground of sentiment, its audience is heterogeneous, the good it does is almost incalculable in its power.

Bollywood, its denizens love to say, is one of the places where there is no communal taint. This must be read against their denial that the casting couch exists. It took the public shooting of film producer and music magnate Gulshan Kumar to get them to admit that the criminal underworld had a role in film financing. Critical self-examination is not their strong suit.

Bollywoodians also claim that they are a force in maintaining sectarian equilibrium. For instance, Amitabh Bachchan has often claimed that

Bollywood has had a role in maintaining communal harmony. In a January 2009 interview, the 66-year-old film actor noted how

> Bihar records the maximum crime but has less movie halls. Andhra Pradesh has the maximum movie theatres. It is the movies that keep communal harmony as people of all communities and religion sit together in the hall to watch a movie [...] where they laugh together, weep together... ("Oscars not ultimate recognition", website).

While one is not sure whether one can make such an easy equation between the number of cinema halls and violent crime, Bachchan has pointed to the fact that Bollywood is a shared space. While no language-based cinema can ever claim to be India's national pop culture, Hindi films made in Mumbai seem to have achieved as much of that status as is possible in a nation with 22 national languages and uncounted dialects. Turn to a Malayalam channel playing an *antakshari* (singing game) and no one bats an eyelid, not the host, not the other contestants, not the audience, when a young woman begins singing the anthemic song from *Yaadon ki Baaraat* (Nasir Hussain, 1973), "Chura liya hai tumne jo dil ko".

Part of this is the magic of music. Part of it is the size of the monolith, the way in which Bollywood's faces are recognisable by virtue of the power of repetition, its music the white noise of the nation. Part of it is the way in which popular culture reaches out to us at some level beneath the conscious and defines who we are. Hindi cinema has been defining India for a long time. And for decades, it defined India as an inclusive space where Hindu, Muslim, Sikh and Christian coexist and respect each other's faiths.

In *Khoon Pasina* (Rakesh Kumar, 1977), the film opens on a pair of young male friends, Aslam and Shiva. Aslam is also known as Shera and Shiva is also known as Tiger. Some local boys knock Aslam's skullcap off but it is Shera who demands that they pick it up. Both boys join hands, literally and figuratively, to avenge this act of disrespect to religion. In the aforementioned *Purab aur Pachchim,* the opening scenes of the film are set in Allahabad during a rainstorm and a flood of water, perhaps from the Ganga which runs through the city. As the colonial police hunt a *desh bhakt* (freedom fighter), we see a picture of Vasudev bearing Krishna above his head and crossing the Yamuna, fall to the ground. It is a Muslim man, some uncredited extra, who picks up the picture and holds it to his heart. He excoriates the policemen who have just shot the freedom fighter and gives his life to preserve the image. The epigraph of this essay comprises lines sung at the beginning of the film. One could take this to be a re-statement of the old myth that everything was invented in India first; or could this be a way of saying that Christians and Muslims and Buddhists and Hindus are all flesh of the flesh?

For popular culture in general and Bollywood in particular does not work with careful attention to fact and detail. Instead, it uses the symbolic act, the flourish rich in meaning. To Manoj Kumar, it probably did not matter that Mohammed and Jesus were born in lands that have never been described as Bharat or that the Bible and the Quran cannot be described as homegrown products. Nor did it matter to Manmohan Desai how blood transfusions take place. At one point, early in *Amar Akbar Anthony* (Manmohan Desai, 1977), three young men come to a public hospital to donate blood to an elderly, blind flower seller (Nirupa Roy). The three young men lie down in beds, each one parallel to the next and the first parallel to the old lady. Nurses ask them their names and they say "Amar" (Vinod Khanna), "Akbar" (Rishi Kapoor) and "Anthony" (Amitabh Bachchan) respectively. The blood begins to flow from their arms and into a common tube from where it flows to the old lady. Someone pointed out to Desai that this was not how blood transfusion would take place in a hospital. The three young men would have blood drawn from their veins and stored in bags. These bags would be taken to the blood bank. They would then be exchanged for blood that had already been donated. Desai said that neither he nor his audiences cared for the way in which blood banks actually operated. (Many of them probably knew, since there was an old Bollywood legend which said that blood donation spiked in the week before a Manmohan Desai release. In the 1970s, before AIDS, blood banks paid for blood donations and one could get a ticket in the stalls for 400 millilitres.)

In other words, he was playing with the symbolic reality, entering into a pact with his audience. For we, who were sitting in the theatre, knew that the old lady was the mother of the three boys from whom she had been parted when they were children. We know that they are repaying their debt to her and should we have forgotten, the soundtrack reminds us with "*Kya iski keemat chukaani nahin? / Khoon khoon hota hai paani nahin.*" On another level, this can also be read as the three communities paying their debt to the motherland.

This construction of the nation as the sum of its religious communities was not a new project. The patriarchs of the studio age and even those of the 1950s were sure of their position in the world. The masses were illiterate and in need of uplift; cinema was the medium that reached where no other could go, and it was, therefore, their duty to use celluloid to educate and to build, out of India's disparate religious communities and castes, one nation.

Many of the Golden Age filmmakers were well-read men. Some like Mehboob Khan were illiterate but that did not stop them from being cosmopolitan and well informed. The presence of the progressive writers, the *tarakkipasand* (progressive) Urdu poets and the Hindi modern novelists often mediated their own baser and more commercial instincts.

For instance, the combination of Raj Kapoor and Khwaja Ahmed Abbas produced some outstanding cinema through the 1950s and 1960s. When the Hindu Kapoor and the Muslim Abbas worked together, their films glued the punters to their seats while talking about issues like homelessness, poverty, child labour, and socialism. When they went their separate ways, Abbas became a demagogue and Kapoor began to turn out cinema that relied on wet women rather than burning issues.

These men would have known that the young nation's primary challenge was extinguishing the flames of Partition and starting the process of living together again. To this end, therefore, the Muslim figures in Hindi cinema were always presented in a kindly light. Rahim Chacha was the good guy in the *basti* in innumerable films. It is Abdul Rashid (Manmohan Krishna) who adopts the orphan and swears to bring it up as a human being in *Dhool ka Phool* (Yash Chopra, 1959). In *Sholay* (Ramesh Sippy, 1975), the imam (A.K. Hangal) does not regret the loss of his son (Sachin); instead he says it is time for his prayers and that he will now go and ask Allah why he was not given more sons to lose for the village.

And while some of this may be imputed to a genuine desire to be inclusive, it was not always an honest impulse. Some part of it was pure commerce. The native Urdu speaker, the Muslim, was a natural part of the Hindi film audience and he could not be alienated. The native English speaker on the other hand could be mocked. Christians, therefore, turned up as morally degenerate figures; their women smoked and drank and were called Lily and Rosy; the men gambled and were small-time hoods called Robert and Rocky. Parsis too were fair game since, like the Christians, they largely preferred Western cinema. Thus the prototype Parsi woman was the sex-starved and inquisitive Mrs. Pestonji (Piloo Wadia) in *Bobby*; the prototype Parsi male was the effeminate and hysterical man into whose car Feroze Khan bumps in *Qurbani* (Feroz Khan, 1980).

Tribal India? Basing oneself on Bollywood, one might assume that all of them are cannibals who worship totems, shout hurrr-hurrr and want to cook the heroine in a stew pot.

Dalit India? Not many films come to mind: Franz Osten's *Achhut Kanya* (1936), Bimal Roy's *Sujata* (1959), in which Nutan plays a low-caste girl; Ashutosh Gowariker's *Lagaan* (2001), in which one of the players has the name Kachrya. (There was also *Aarakshan* (Prakash Jha, 2011) but that was about the issue of reservations and caste-based politics.) *Souten* (Saawan Kumar Tak, 1983) is the only film that I can think of in which one of the characters has an actual hatred of the low-caste. Rukmini (Tina Munim) has an almost visceral revulsion for the Dalits played by Shriram Lagoo and Padmini Kolhapure. All these roles demand sympathy for the Dalit characters, but that only four or five films come to mind in a cinema that has been around for more than a hundred years is indicative.

In terms of the making of the nation, it was emphasised that unity was strength and that this unity had to stretch beyond the religious. The symbolism was often crude. In *Five Rifles* (1974), I.S. Johar's bizarre film, a king of some Cloudcuckoostan has three images in glittering rhinestones that must be kept safe to ensure that the country is safe. One is Krishna playing his flute, the other is a cross and the third is the name of Allah in Arabic. One might argue that *Five Rifles* was a C-grade film but the crudeness extended across genres. *Naseeb* (1981), for instance, had a multi-star cast led by Amitabh Bachchan, Hema Malini, Reena Roy, Rishi Kapoor and Shatrughan Sinha (in alphabetical order, as the posters said). For some reason, Amitabh goes by the name John Jaani Janardhan. In the middle of a song celebrating the golden jubilee of *Dharam Veer* (1977), another Desai superhit, Bachchan sings a song to entertain the stars. In the course of it, someone asks him how it is that he has three names?

Extra: *Ek aadmi ke teen naam kaise?*
JJJ (sings): *Yeh teenon naam hai mere…*
He goes to a window and points.
JJJ: *Allah…*
Outside it, a mosque lights up.
JJJ: *…Jesus…*
Outside the next window, a church lights up
JJJ: *…Ram hai mere…*
Outside the third window, a temple lights up.

This may explain what Shah Rukh Khan means when he says, "I have Allah and Om in my room. Karan [Johar] says it's like a Hindi film" (Bhattacharya 2003, quoting from Pradhan 2003).

But even if it was crude, it was valuable in a way that we did not notice. Not until it suddenly went away. In the 1990s, Bollywood went Hindu. The Hindu wedding became the focus of several films. The film title, always rendered in three languages (Roman, Devnagri and Urdu), was suddenly down to two scripts and no prizes for guessing which one was dropped. *Gadar: Ek Prem Katha* was released and went on to be a mega success, perhaps even the apotheosis of the anti-Muslim film.

Because a few years after that, the Muslim figure came back. This seemed a little surprising but then once again, commercial arithmetic may have had something to do with it. The United Kingdom market is now a significant factor in the success or failure of a Hindi film. At a median price of eight pounds sterling for a new release, each Briton of Pakistani origin or of Indian Muslim origin who hears that a film has unflattering representations of his community is a valuable commodity.

In some senses, this does not matter.

In the world of the imagination, there are many things that play out differently from the way things happen in the streets. This means that the man who weeps at "*Arre ruk jaa re bande*" (Hey human, just hold on) may still go out with a mob, a *mashaal* (burning torch) in his hand. But the only way to defend the inclusive, the only way to support the notion of a plural State, is to repeat it again and again. To say that there is no other way. To say that we have to learn to live together. To say that when the blood flows, you cannot tell by its colour where it came from. That the earth has no religion.

That man is born into humanity and not into a religion. That the rainbow is made of many more colours than we can imagine.

When this becomes part of the popular imagination, when we are ashamed of how we "Other" each other on the basis of what we eat and what we worship, when we can segregate the fanatic and the sectarian, one is fairly sure that social scientists of every stripe will be forced to look at the role popular culture had to play in how this consensus developed.

The Way To Go

Sanjukta Dasgupta

"It's a boy, it's a boy," the women helping the midwife cheered. The slightly-built woman, who lay on her back on a low bed, gasped and let the perspiration flowing out of her pores cool her now relaxed body.

Saraju gestured to the woman closest to her to show her the baby. She stretched her arm and placed her hand on a head of jet-black hair, tears rose in her eyes as she murmured, "*shanti, shanti*". Yes peace at last, she felt she would never again bear another child. Two daughters followed by a son was more than enough family for her frail frame to care for.

"No not Shanti, we will call him Arjun after the supreme archer of the Mahabharata, the soulmate of Lord Krishna," said her husband, who of course, was always right.

So Saraju's Shanti, a whispered name between mother and son, Manindra Gupta's son Arjun, came to the world where he would reside for the next eight decades, without however a single idea in his mind just then, but a great hunger that his doting mother attended to, nursing him laughingly, as she rocked him against her bosom. In the evenings, she held him up and pointed out the mellow moon and the twinkling stars.

Many, many years later when schoolmaster Arjun held his own daughter in his arms and whispered her name for the first time in her ear, the one face that rose in his mind's screen was that of his mother Saraju. He turned towards her.

Standing next to him in the hospital, Saraju was waiting to welcome her granddaughter. She gathered the little one with a head full of curly hair in her arms and said, "She looks like Saraswati." Saraswati, the Hindu Goddess of Learning.

Arjun's wife Meena thought Saraswati was a very appropriate name, and wondered how her illiterate mother-in-law could think of such a name for her granddaughter.

But Arjun said very gently, "No mother, I'll call her Indira."

His wife Meena laughed, "Inspired by Jawaharlal Nehru, I'm sure. But Nehru's Indira was privileged."

"So what," retorted Arjun. "I may not be as affluent or aristocratic, but we are blue-blooded poor Vaidyas. I'll give her the best of education and then let's see."

In Bengal, the Vaidyas were traditionally regarded to be second in line to the Brahmins in the caste hierarchy. Arjun loved to flaunt his Vaidya caste. His friends even joked that Arjun was a Marxist Vaidya, a bizarre oxymoron.

Meena taught in the same school as Arjun. From colleagues to friendship, then love and marriage.

When Arjun admitted Indira to the local English medium Roman Catholic Convent School, there was universal consternation. "Imagine a freedom fighter admitting his daughter to an English medium school. She will become a Christian surely and inevitably a misfit."

But Meena supported Arjun completely.

Indira fell in love with the English language. She wrote poems and stories in English. She sang English songs. She recited passages from Shakespeare's *Macbeth* and *Julius Caesar.* Arjun was thrilled. His daughter Indira Gupta's English poems were now being published in the *The Statesman.*

"Terrible, these are not poems. Just a way of insulting the mother-tongue," folks thundered.

Arjun smiled and told teenaged Indira, "The Goddess of Learning Saraswati is a secular Goddess. Ignore the politics of language."

"A secular Goddess," Indira laughed. Her tinkling laughter mingled with the gentle boom of her father's guffaw.

Indira knew with such a father she could never go wrong.

Caught in Contradictions: India Today

Premila Paul

Until her retirement Premila Paul taught literatures in English at the American College, Madurai, and she has published on Indian literature and gender issues.

*Dr. Paul was a founding member and is currently Associate Director of the renowned Study Centre for Indian Literature in English and Translation (*SCILET*).*

What makes India a fascinating place to visit, to dream of and also to live in are strangely the inherent paradoxes, contradictions and an order in chaos that assures a place for every strand of culture and people of all persuasions. A well-orchestrated life and utter noiselessness do not interest Indians. People-noise is routine music that energises and binds people and gives them a strong sense of community. While celebrating the newspaper *Times of India*'s 175th anniversary of circulation, Jug Suraiya referred to this phenomenon as "creative chaos" in the "world's biggest—and loudest—democracy" (April 24th, 2013, 2).

India, large and loud, continues to thrive between the pulls of modern outlook and medieval mindset. Forces of progression and regression take a toll on Indian society simultaneously, representing a glorious contradiction. Thus centuries seem to coexist in India. What is true for one region / community is not true for another.

The onslaught of globalisation has further sharpened the existing contradictions. There is a strong Indian presence in the IT industry around the globe but it is a fact that India has the largest population of illiterates in the world, and a disproportionate number of them are women. There are more women in medical schools than men but strong preference for a son and dowry harassment continue unabated. Abortion may be unlawful but pro-choice abounds in practice and is even seen as a humane solution to population growth. India has been a model nation in establishing non-violence as the most powerful means to an end. But sporadic violence in India has tarnished its image. It is in the state of Kerala in India that a Communist Party came to power through the electoral process for the first time in the world. But Communism glorified as the ideal to establish societal egalitarianism has been betrayed by feudal minds breaking the party into splintered groups. A few Indians invariably figure in *Time* magazine's annual list of the richest in Asia but 35 per cent of the population is said to live below the poverty line. While middle-class women, their flaws and failures come under minute scrutiny, people gladly condone major drawbacks in political figures and deify them.

Globalisation promotes a kind of sameness, a mall consumerism of branded products. But an aggressive drive to maintain and regularise the supply of ethnic products also runs parallel in India. There is equal demand for both markets. The immense local popularity and critical international recognition that the film *Kaakka Muttai* enjoyed, shows how even the poor slum dwellers do not escape the lure of consumerism, a direct impact of globalisation. Pizza is the metaphor for desire planted in the poor by globalisation. Gratification of the global leads ultimately to privileging of the local, native and the familiar. Rooted in tradition, one is better equipped to absorb the best from other ways of life.

Closed minds, ill-equipped to respond to the inescapable changes flooding their lives 24/7 through the media and Internet, seek desperate assurance in the familiar and the known. Their insecurity urges them to reaffirm their sense of self / community by reviving rituals and religious practices. They aggressively reclaim all that is old, relevant or otherwise, to counter and slow down the pace of change. They also take refuge in jingoistic rhetoric. India has all along been proud of its inheritance of diversity and its absorptive capacity. Insistence on cultural purity and debates on pollution possibilities tend to erode the very Indian value base and make a mockery of the great Indian heritage.

When hierarchical power positions are challenged by new ways of life, there is a concerted effort to lay boundaries, tighten divisions, and attribute the cause of all dislocations and disturbances to Western influence. Feminism, for instance, is a Western bomb that would destabilise and destroy the sacred institution of the Indian family. The women's rights movement to eradicate anti-female atrocities was active in India long before the term "feminism" was popularised in the West. Confident of impunity, the culture fanatics could incite mob frenzy and disrupt whatever is feared as a threat or inconvenience to their authority, like the shooting of Deepa Mehta's film *Water*. The cruel custom of child marriage that the film exposes is interpreted as the West's attempt to defame Hinduism. Vandalism is periodically unleashed on traders and customers who cash in on Valentine's Day celebrations.

Indians place a high premium on culture and religion. Religions as practised in India have both a salubrious and detrimental effect on the collective psyche of the people. Animosities and riots erupt only because of the appropriation of religions by politicians for their personal gain, as in the recent violent case of diet politics. No other country mixes religion with politics as India does to the extent of depriving it totally of spirituality. In vote bank politics, political leaders sport religious markers to show their oneness with a particular religious community. Even disaster management sites provide ample photo opportunities with certain communities for political use later during elections.

Most Hindus in India had a sense of humour about representations of their deities before politicians turned self-appointed culture-protectors. The hounding of India's own renowned artist, M.F. Hussain, vandalism of his art exhibition and his subsequent self-imposed exile are all a disgrace that India has to live with, and remember not to repeat. Instances of intolerance towards films, books, writers, people of other ethnicity, exclusivity, cultural righteousness, all in the name of preserving Indian culture seem to be increasing day by day. That is certainly a matter of deep concern and alarming anxiety for average Indians, who believe strongly in the inclusive great Indian civilisation. Their daily routine involves people of all religions and cultures. The killing of rationalists like Govind Pansare, Narendra Dabholkar and M.M. Kalburgi has caused deep anguish and helplessness in well-meaning Indians.

While the move to promote Indian languages is to be appreciated, any attempt to edge English out will render Indian youth immobile, less qualified and even unemployable in the global market. What the politicians fail to acknowledge is that English is not just an international language but also an inter-state link language within India. But these politicians who preach the "Be Indian" message to the gullible masses make sure that their own children are educated in the best, elite English medium schools in the country or overseas. Differences that abound in India are religion-, region-, caste-, language- and ethnicity-based. These are valuable cultural components that enhance the vibrancy of the land. But the parochialists manipulate these differences as divisions. We have to consciously weed out the divisionist forces, because there is potential here for xenophobia.

Post-Partition, Muslims were subjected to the worst kind of profiling, and since 9/11, this has received tacit approval from the international community. At times of border tensions and cricket matches, Indian Muslims are wrongly accused of disloyalty. Extremism is not the exclusive prerogative of any one religion, and the more austere practices of every religion usually include a lunatic fringe. But we tend to associate this with certain other religions and refuse to acknowledge its presence in our own. Hate propaganda itself is a brand of terrorism that spreads fear and enmity but remains unchecked by law.

Even after the horror of Partition, Hindus, Sikhs and Muslims have found ways to live together in amity and peace. But in the last two to three decades there have been a string of horror stories: the demolition of the Babri Masjid (1992), the Bombay riots (1992), the attack on the Indian Parliament (2001), the Godhra incident and the Gujarat violence that followed it (2002), the assault on the iconic Hotel Taj (2008), and that is just to mention the better-known events. There is now a general reluctance to acknowledge the identities of Muslims beyond their religion. He or she is a Muslim and not a Rajasthani, as if religion had displaced him / her from ethnicity and region, whereas for Hindus four identities—religious, regional, linguistic, and professional—are rightfully theirs. When accusations against Muslims gather steam, they experience a heightened self-consciousness and take on an identity they have never felt before. They tend to promote the stereotypical image of a Muslim with external trappings, thus compressing their identity into the narrow confines of religion.

Muslims themselves are culturally diverse. A Kerala Muslim has culturally more in common with a Hindu or Christian Keralite than with a Bihari or Bengali Muslim. A Punjabi Hindu has culturally more in common with a Punjabi Muslim than with a Tamil Hindu. Cultural and linguistic identities often prove to be stronger than their religious identity even for Bengalis and Bangladeshis.

The religious worship that people end up practising in India is a concoction of rituals drawn from different religions. Unless one is a fanatic convinced of one's religious superiority, everybody ends up celebrating everybody else's festivals. Just as Deepavali means lighting fire crackers with friends of all religions, Ramzan involves sharing of Biriyani with non-Muslim friends, and Christmas is a time for cake distribution to non-Christian friends. Faith may be personal but the celebration of festivals is inclusive and social.

Some religious celebrations are planned in such a way as to bring people of different faiths together. There are Hindu functions where Muslims play hosts; there are Hindu pilgrimages where Muslims maintain rest stops. There are annual Hindu festivals that replay and perform legends that involve Muslims.

Many Muslim rulers supported Hindu temples and Hindu art with generous grants in the past. The famous Vaishnava Srirangam Temple in Tiruchirappalli received such patronage from the Arcot nawabs. Though non-Hindus are not allowed into the *sanctum sanctorum* enclosure of the temple, the Tanjore painting of Thulukka Nachiyar, the Muslim consort of Lord Vishnu, finds a legitimate place inside. During the Vaikunda Ekadasi festival in December—January, Lord Vishnu is taken in a ceremonial procession to the Muslim consort, whom he is supposed to serve for ten days.

Legends of Hindu-Muslim interaction and co-operation abound. There have been soul-stirring instances of Muslims sheltering Hindus, Hindus protecting Muslims and Christians giving refuge to Sikhs during instigated riots. The poor in particular have proved time and again that nurturing animosity is a futile luxury that they cannot afford.

The ten-day annual festival in the Velankanni Basilica of our Lady of Good Health, Tamil Nadu (referred to as the "Lourdes of the East"), is the best example of millions of pilgrims of all religious affiliations coming together for worship in India. The Holy Catholic Mass is conducted in at least eight languages. The dynamic forms of worship in and around the church accommodate rituals of all religious and folk traditions.

Saba Naqvi's book *In Good Faith: A Journey in Search of an Unknown India* (2012) gives a fascinating account of a number of multi-religious forms of worship and multi-cultural ways of living in different parts of contemporary India as a counter to the fundamentalism that coexists. Ashis Nandy states in the blurb that this book will

> re-educate those academics who glibly use hollowed-out political slogans like inter-faith dialogue, religious tolerance, syncretism and secularism. It shows that we live in a land where such a dialogue has been going on, silently and inconspicuously, in front of our eyes and within our earshot for centuries. Only we did not want to listen or to see.

India is a unique nation that still assigns spaces in a big way to minorities. Though there are advantages and disadvantages to this special consideration / encouragement, Indian democracy encourages diversity with token gestures. Indian Muslims have a secure place in Indian democracy. An Indian Muslim can still hope to be a cricket captain, dominate the film world like the Khan-triumvirate, or even become President or Vice President of India.

There have been occasional tensions between Hindus and Christians too, often because of the moral superiority assumed by Christian evangelical preachers that they alone are in the know-how of salvation. Rival interpretations of the Bible and of Christ abound even within Christianity. Each sect of Christianity believes that its own brand of Christianity is above criticism. Such fundamentalist Christians are eager to proselytise not only Hindus, Sikhs or Muslims, but even other Christians whose liberal / secular beliefs happen to fall outside the parameters of their narrow brand of Christianity.

History illustrates that criticism is vital to the growth of religions and God cannot be weakened by criticism. Firm faith in a particular religion need not make a person a better human being; nor does questioning its relevance make a person evil. Hinduism's great strength has been its freedom of thought. Buddha, Guru Nanak and Mahavira were all critics of Hindu thought and practices. They are accepted as reformer–critics in the accommodative Hindu tradition. A religion not challenged or analysed is a static one. Despite political attempts to make gods instruments of polarisation, the polytheistic tradition and pluralistic ethos of most of the Hindus have equipped them to handle criticism of their forms of worship better than the Christians and Muslims.

The recent belligerence of political parties that promote Hindu fundamentalism has subdued the loud moral self-righteousness of Christian evangelical preachers. Christians form less than 2.3 per cent of the Indian population. Yet their presence is keenly felt because of institutions established by the early Christian missionaries that have served people for more than a century in the education and health sectors. Now there is a welcome mushrooming of good secular and non-Christian institutions run by individuals and philanthropic trusts. But still some of the best institutions of higher learning in the country are Christian.

Education is power and power is both despised and desired. Accusations of elitism, minoritism and not being Indian enough are mounted against these institutions. Yet it is a fact that they seek out first-generation learners and were the first in the country to open their portals to the underprivileged and marginalised sections of society. History records that some of these educational institutions not only actively supported the Indian freedom movement but also sheltered freedom fighters. A sizable number of people from marginalised, disadvantaged communities embraced Christianity and became beneficiaries of the social amelioration schemes during the colonial days. Christians today from both the privileged and underprivileged sections of society have easier access to quality education from some of the best institutions in the country. The Syrian Christians of Kerala are a privileged lot, mobile and entrepreneurial, and have made a big mark in every field in India. Christians are seen as a threat no longer because of their evangelism but because of their definite place in the field of education.

Some of the Christian institutions have set high standards of liberal education while government-run institutions fail to maintain even basic standards. Overseas church support makes them centres of privilege, and they focus on liberalising and broadening the scope of the learning process in a way that has nothing to do with religious conversion. However, this is a matter of resentment for many average Indians who have no access to such plum education. It is ironic that some products of elite liberal Christian centres of higher learning have emerged as national leaders promoting fundamentalist Hindu political ideologies. While they acknowledge and attribute their growth to these centres of excellence, they have no qualms about unlearning the liberal education that they received. Their outlook is anything but liberal.

The burning down of churches, the vandalising of their libraries, and the rape of nuns in Kolkata and Odisha are all expressions of sheer envy and frustration, and not a reaction to any proselytisation drive. Even under the British Raj, the strength of the Christian population did not go up considerably. Religious conversions of the underprivileged happen because of their frustration with a community that has failed them. The Ghar Wapsi programme, claimed to be a mass re-conversion drive, is ironically a desperate but poor imitation of what fundamentalist Hindus attack the Christians for supposedly doing. Return to the original faith involves a typical purification ceremony with fire and water. Again, the targets for re-conversion are the underprivileged Dalits and tribals.

At times, the media indulge in stereotypical depictions of Christians—liquor-serving families, girls flaunting Western attire, young people in relaxed relationships with members of the opposite sex. In films, cabaret dancers and honey traps often bear Western or Christian names, and sport neck chains with crosses. In India, most men, whatever their religion might be, are in Western clothes, but women wearing comfortable Western clothes are morally suspect. In real life, Christians are accused of leading a life of deviation from the norm of Indianness. From non-vegetarianism to their attire, Indian Christians are blamed for aping the West.

It is true that a Western educational system, with curricula imposed on Indians since colonial times, has encouraged anglophilia among Indians. All Indian minds need to be decolonised, not just those of Indian Christians. We make a fetish of British pronunciation, and insist on students memorising Shakespeare soliloquies. Educational standards are always set by the West. We accuse the West of inflicting its influence on Indians, but feel superior because of that very connection. Sometimes our self-esteem is linked to our ability to converse freely in English. We are caught in contradictions between resenting anything that is associated with the colonial power and also desperately wanting to be modern like the West. Modernity and development for an average Indian is Westernisation.

Religion is often identified with a geographical location. Christianity is not a Western religion and had taken root in India long before the British colonised the land. Yet it is seen as a Western religion because it was practised and propagated by the colonisers, whose ways were both admired and hated by the colonised. Indian culture will embrace a daughter-in-law, claiming her as its own and a blessed inclusion to the family. But it often honours her with responsibility rather than power. Once she wields power, even a Sonia Gandhi, the celebrated "Sonia bahu", will be dubbed an "alien Italian Christian". Being Christian becomes an accusation, not part of one's identity as an Indian. It is power that is both desired and despised.

The Indian contradiction is best demonstrated in Indian attitudes towards women. Here all differences and divisions between religions / ideologies happily collapse. A family's honour is defined through women, who have to represent all that is good in tradition. But films and other media objectify women as sex dolls; women are made to dance suggestively in scanty clothes for popular consumption and are projected as objects of pleasure.

A woman is venerated as goddess in both the benign and destructive forms, Parvati and Kali. But she is also harassed on every street corner, and in homes and work places. The oppressive practices against women are justified in the name of culture and they are invested with the burden of preserving a hoary culture. Though Gandhi was a strong advocate of women's rights, by eulogising women's virtues and presenting them as symbols of sacrifice and strength, he set high standards for them and denied them their right to be human.

When women defy the norms set for them, crossing the *Lakshman Rekha*s (strict conventions) drawn for them, they become targets of moral policing. When there is a problem, it is the women who are put in a cage for protection and the offenders who go scot free. Strict dress codes and curfews are for women and not for the habitual male offenders. So in Indian culture, a woman is in a denial / self-denial trap. She either stands for sacrifice and selflessness or she represents total abandonment to the senses. Trapped in societal expectations, she is either sacred or profane but never human.

Hinduism has an ambivalent attitude to woman, to dance, and to sex. It flaunts its celebration of sex through art as a route to realisation of God within but it is also prudish about sex. A woman dancer entices man to experience sexual energy, the energy of life / creation which is actually the realisation of the divine. Reaching the plane of spiritual consciousness is possible through a woman / dancer. But her role is minimised and limited to being an instrument. Dance as an art form has sacred intent but the dancer's use of the body is a seductive act and, therefore, base. A dancer is at once a priestess and a seductress. Dance is at once sacred and profane. The experience of it is both mundane and mysterious.

Homologous with this are the blatant contradictions in the Indian attitude to sex. Sex has the status of performing art, as illustrated in the erotic temple sculptures of Khajuraho and Konark. There is no trace of repression. As Gurcharan Das (2015) has written:

> If creation begins with light in the Judeo-Christian tradition of the West (when God says "let there be light"), in India it begins with *kama*, "desire" [...]. Early on, ancient Indians understood that *kama* is the source of creation, procreation and, indeed, all action [...]. They even created an intoxicating deity in its name and built a charming mythology around it.

It is ironic that the land that inspired the *Kamasutra* has proposed to block pornographic websites in the name of curbing rapist tendencies: the world's largest democracy attempting to control illegitimate population growth in the century of techno-geeks? Realising its inability to censor cyberspace, however, the government quickly reversed its stand. Elected representatives have been caught watching pornography in assembly sessions. Some politicians condone rapes as "boys making mistakes" and even place the blame squarely on women who dare to stay out late or venture out alone. The provocative dances and close-ups of the female body limit women's power over their own bodies. The erotic and the ascetic coexist in the Indian collective psyche. But projecting them as binaries and making a virtue of sexual abstinence, however Gandhian that might be, indicates a mental obsession with sex.

Contradictions in the Indian psyche continue to beget more contradictions. Variations of repressive social practices have even invaded cyberspace and operate through virtual means. Honour killings and rape as punishment are meted out by social entities like the *khap panchayat*s (gatherings of village elders). What is most disturbing and depressing are the apathy of the police and the habitual silence of the State. Is it the State's abdication of responsibility or does the State nonchalantly provide impunity to the offenders? Is India a progressive nation or a decadent civilisation? The signals are hard to read.

We cannot help but share the apprehensions of Nayantara Sahgal, who articulates the fear that "The idea of India is at stake" and that "the State has brought an iron curtain down on the freedom of thought" (Us Salam, 2015). The scope for dissent is diminishing in the politically charged climate. Sensible debates are systematically being stifled and State-sponsored regimented thinking is being promoted through the revision of school curricula and the rewriting of history.

However, all is not lost. India is no failed State. Democracy still functions, despite all attempts at intimidation. We still have a free press, an independent judiciary and a very vibrant civil society. The fundamental, secular spirit of India will surely survive the sectarian designs of politicians. We are grateful that the deliberately fostered divisions among us crumble whenever there is a true call of humanity. For every instance of bigotry, we have any number of instances to show that Indians truly value and celebrate their differences and cherish their shared roots and the shared cultural denominators that bind them. They are well aware that valorisation of the differences could lead to divisions and ghettoisation. Obsession with the Other can lead to extremism. Coexistence is possible without opposition. And there is a far deeper respect for the secular spirit of India that is enshrined in our Constitution than the sectarians can possibly imagine.

This was seen in the spontaneous outpouring of affection that A.P.J. Abdul Kalam, India's 11th President, received from every part of India and the outpouring of grief from the young and old of every section of society at his death on July 27th, 2015. His accessibility endeared him to people who continued to look up to him as a role model long after he had laid down office. A much sought-after teacher by students of all age groups, from school children to business graduates to technocrats, he played his teacher role most effectively, literally till he breathed his last.

Born a Muslim, Abdul Kalam's sensitive exposure to and interactions with practitioners of other faiths right from childhood helped him inherit and internalise a truly secular tradition. As Shashi Tharoor (2015) has pointed out:

> In melding the Islam into which he was born with a strong sense of the traditions in which his civilisation was anchored, Abdul Kalam was a complete Indian, an embodiment of the eclecticism of India's heritage of diversity.

Kalam represented and lived the very idea and ideal of India. With his "Vision 2020" and "What-Can-I-Give Movement," he inspired the young to do the very best and realise their full potential. This made him a youth icon at 83, in life and in death.

Purity of a caste, race, culture or religion is a myth. Exclusivity is impossible. Definitions of purity are bound to be subjective. Cultures travel, cross borders, mingle with other cultures and return altered. Culture is not a static structure, but is ever-evolving. In our attempt to understand and define culture in terms of our own immediate background and upbringing, some forget the vibrant sub-cultures and amazing diversity that India is proud of and which other countries are envious of.

Though not yet an economic power, India has become a model nation with its warm acceptance of diverse cultures and multiple identities. Gandhian *ahimsa* (non-violence) is not merely a passive resistance to colonial power but an active reaching out to people of other cultures. Gandhism is more relevant than ever in contemporary India, to secularise every religion and counter the hegemonising drive, enabling all citizens of every persuasion to walk tall as proud Indians.

India from the Outside—A Personal View

T.W. Geraghty

T.W. Geraghty is an Irish writer, teacher, traveller and intercultural commentator, who has been visiting India for almost half a century.

Geraghty has been able, he says, to observe how much the country has changed during that time but also how much India is still being held back.

So—what is this place India all about? Take up a position somewhere in the crowded heart of an Indian city (not in the middle of the road, naturally), and watch the people carefully. Or *try* to, because you'll not have much peace to only stand and stare. You'll be swept up by what you experience: visually, by a whirl of colours, fabrics, beards and hairstyles, jewellery, and shades of skin; olfactorily, by a clutch of smells, exotic or oppressive—see the wonderful description of the street smells of Calcutta in Ved Mehta's *Portrait of India* (1970, 403–4), the account heightened, if anything, by the author's blindness; haptically, too, as you are jostled, though mostly in a good-natured manner; and aurally, by the buzz of different languages and by the many tones of voice. You may find yourself asking: what are all these people *doing*? But if you focus on only one person, or on one interaction, you'll soon be distracted by what is happening nearby.

Nor will you be left alone, as you might normally expect to be in downtown London, Paris or New York. Someone will try to sell you something. If you're a conventionally-dressed male Westerner like myself, a helpful gentleman might even offer to lead you to an amenable young woman, or (if you decline) to a friendly young man eager to make your acquaintance, or (refusing to give up on you) mention that he could provide you with some indispensable accessory for your digital camera or your Smart phone, or help you in changing your money. And would you by any chance happen to need the assistance of an experienced guide? (Female Westerners, and hippies, are apparently offered a slightly different range of commodities and services.)

Even if by waving a magic wand you could freeze everyone, and investigate each of them in turn and at your leisure, you'd still get a headache trying to work out how the pieces of the puzzle fit together. All those castes and ethnic and religious groups, with their varying loyalties, commitments, styles, and ways of doing things, and all of them managing, somehow, to share a city.

Western travellers to India have been reporting such experiences and feelings for a long time. For some, it can be overwhelming. Sally Belfrage (1981), for instance, wrote:

> The first view of urban India is surely the worst in the world. It can never again be so shocking; one could never again survive the repetition of its first assault on the senses. The degradation and the hopeless hordes are so beyond the worst expectations that there is no armour, no protection possible (quoted in Pigott-Smith 1986, 49).

Less gloomily, Trevor Grove, on a cultural tour of Northern India in 1986 with a group of "youngish teachers and spry pensioners" from Britain, describes Chandni Chowk in Old Delhi, where he also had a meeting, similar to mine, with a helpful, commercially-minded gentleman:

> Here [in the bazaar] you encounter the many-headed monster itself, the endless, churning throng whose composite face is the face of modern India. Carried on this flood of buying, selling, betel-chewing, betel-spitting, importuning, chattering, menacing, smiling humanity is a flotsam of rickshaws, bicycles and cars whose bells and horns add to the din. "Sir, Sir, you want pyjamas, Indian shirt, young girl, change money, what your good name, Sir?" (6).

My own experience as described at the beginning of this essay wasn't in Delhi, but in Mumbai (or Bombay, as it was still called when I first started going there). Mumbai isn't India, of course, and that kind of diversity in one place is the exception rather than the rule. I've always felt that, despite the poverty, despite the slums, despite the chasing after money (or maybe because of it?), Mumbai is a special case, a city of hope. Delhi, to my mind, rather less so: they chase after money there, too, but as part of the infernal trio of cash, power and status (and if you get your hands on just one of those, the other two will often follow).

Nevertheless, if we take Mumbai as a model of baffling but positive social interaction, there are little Mumbais in the other great cities of India as well, too, islands of day-to-day compromise and social pragmatism. Go out into the countryside or to small-town India, however, and you'll not encounter so much of that willingness to work around rules and differences. What you'll find is a lot of bone-headed intolerance, and even cruelty. It was that sort of nastiness that, when I was a young man, made me stop going to India for several years.

I remember, for example, a beggar child standing outside a restaurant in New Delhi one evening, holding her baby brother in her arms and asking a tourist for money. Before the tourist could react, an Indian gentleman stepped nimbly forward and smacked the girl across the face so hard that the baby slipped out of her hands and fell on the road; then he turned and apologised to the tourist: "You're a guest in our country, Sir. You shouldn't have to see such people. Indira and Sanjay had the right idea, clearing all that riffraff out of the capital."

I was the tourist. To my abiding shame, I didn't know how to respond.

Funny how "Untouchables" suddenly become touchable when it comes to hitting them (or raping their women).

I remember—in sacred Varanasi, of all places—a horse covered in welts and sores, beaten and slowly dying on its feet but still harnessed to its cart. I thought of that terrible scene in Dostoyevsky's *Brothers Karamazov* where Ivan Karamazov describes a horse being flogged across the eyes. Ivan is quoting from a famous poem by Nekrasov, but he later moves on to describe cruelty to helpless children. "Our historical pastime [in Russia] is the direct satisfaction of inflicting pain," he declares. "But that's only a horse, and God has given [us] horses to be beaten" (264).

Yet despite his callousness, that carter in the holiest city of India was probably not a sadist as we would understand it. No doubt he badly needed the horse, but he was poor, and he had to make the animal work, and he could hardly afford the luxury of spoiling the horse by letting it rest. Besides, if it was suffering, wasn't that simply its karma from the previous life?

And I remember, sadly, a clutch of tattered old ladies cowering outside a school kitchen in Rajasthan, begging for scraps of food. When I asked him about them, the headmaster of the school told me that they were widows, and that they would starve without those handouts, because they were too old to do labouring jobs on the roads or on building sites (if they were to be had), or to sell their bodies. He felt pity for them, certainly, but their families and their former neighbours apparently hadn't. After all, the women had let their husbands die before them—though their husbands may already have been grown men when they married them as child brides—and so they had failed badly in their duty and consequently been thrown out to fend for themselves.

The rules are harsh, and when they are imposed unthinkingly, they leave no room for kindness.

I could have set against those horrors the kindness, generosity and graciousness that I also experienced everywhere that I went in India. But young people have fewer resources of character and experience that they can draw on than the elderly do, and so they tend to panic or overreact under pressure. If I was unfair to India back then, I now regret it.

On the other hand, there is no point in simply ignoring the darker side of Indian life, or denying the country's complexity (and diversity). In 2002, the Government of India launched a huge international publicity campaign to promote India as a tourist destination. But as an online case study of the advertising initiative pointed out:

> Although the "Incredible India" campaign was generally well received, industry observers differed in their opinions on the positioning of India in the campaign. For example, G.S. Murari, Director, Fidelis Advertising and Marketing Pvt. Ltd., said he was uncomfortable with the tagline "Incredible India".
>
> He was of the opinion that since India was not a unidimensional country like Singapore or the Maldives, using a word like "incredible" to describe India as a whole was not appropriate. He argued that a single word could never describe a multi-faceted country like India... (ICMR, website).

Campaigns to promote specific areas of India have also attracted negative attention. For example, the "God's Own Country" campaign to promote foreign tourism to Kerala was recently subjected to media criticism because of the vast numbers of stray dogs roaming about in the state. These were regarded as an eyesore, feared to be a health hazard, and viewed as a potential menace to human beings, and consequently there was a debate about whether or not to cull them (see, for example, Pawar, 2015, website). An online campaign to boycott Kerala tourism was even launched. Embarrassingly, "God" is an anagram of "dog".

The social problems are still there, and yet India has changed a great deal, and it is still changing, because of education and modernisation, because of globalisation and population movement, and because of television, mobile phones and the Internet, all of which expose you to diversity. When your life becomes noticeably better or more interesting, it tends to make you start to reflect. You will still have your rules, but so will they, those others, and you will find yourself accommodating yourself to the situation, just as they will too. You meet new people, and you learn new strategies for living. You begin to question some of the old rules and certainties—or you simply ignore them.

All of which makes you a danger to those who have a vested interest in the old ways. Those people who don't want their complacent "wisdom" to be challenged, for instance, or who don't want to give up their social or economic privileges, or their political power, based on (depending on whichever set of social science terminology you prefer) *ascribed* rather than *achieved status* (Linton 1936), *traditional* rather than *secular–rational authority* (Inglehart 1997), or *status consistency* (Hofstede 1991), a characteristic of *large-power-distance cultures*—of which India is a classic example.

The greatest threat to those vested interests is knowledge and education. Because, armed with knowledge and with education, some brave person may choose to get up and say: "This man is a superstitious fool—and here's the proof!" Or: "No, it isn't necessary, or even advisable, to do it like that. Just take a peep at this website: *that* is how they do it in Somewhere-Else-Istan, or in Distantpur, and wouldn't you agree that it works much better? And look: do you see who's in charge there? His father was a coolie. Or: she's a woman. Or a Muslim. And they're *good*."

Almost more than anyone else, it is arguably a certain Sri Narendra Damodardas Modi, Prime Minister of India, the former *chai-wallah* from the OBC Modh-Ghanchi sub-caste (Mukhopadhyay 2013), who ought to be able to appreciate the idea of upward mobility based on merit. Modi is Hindu, but talent is scarcely a prerogative restricted to the Hindus. India's vast population includes highly gifted individuals from many different groups. It would be tragic if cultural narrow-mindedness, ethnic or religious intolerance, male chauvinism, and fear or hatred of diversity, were allowed to strangle such potential and endanger this wonderful country's progress in the years to come.

Scenes from a Life in Diversity

Jerry Pinto

My friend G is beautiful at sixty-five. She is also bisexual, although she has been married to two men and never regretted either. Last Christmas, she had a celebration.

To it came her gay son, whose name is Imran although he is a Christian by baptism and deeply interested in the Ramayana, and his boyfriend Rishad, who is a Parsi and is a Tycoon-in-Training.

To it came also her Hindu son-in-law and his Christian wife, and their baptised grandchildren.

To it came also her daughter, a devout Muslim who prays five times a day when she can, and her Muslim husband and their three Muslim children.

"That sounds like a set-up for an American playwright who is going to turn this into a tragedy of identity," I say to her.

"Actually, it was a food orgy and everyone got a little drunk and laughed a lot," says G.

~

My mother called the vadapao, Sennerpao.

She meant: Shiv Sena-pao.

This was because the political party called the Shiv Sena is said to have started a series of carts that sold vadapao so that unemployed Maharashtrian youths might make a living.

But stop a moment and look at the composition of the Sennerpao.

The name "pao" itself is Portuguese. The Portuguese taught the Goans to bake and the Goans taught the Muslims to bake and so every bakery worth the pao is run by Muslims. The word is unchanged in Marathi. In the north, they don't know Portuguese, so they call it double-roti.

The potato came to India with the Jesuits who brought it to the Mughal court to present it to Emperor Akbar. So did the chilli, wending its way from Mexico.

The Shiv Sena have made a career out of claiming Maharashtra for the Maharashtrians.

~

I am sitting in Alibag with the poet Imtiaz Dharker, who was Pakistani by birth, British by upbringing, and is married to a Maharashtrian. She is with her second mother-in-law, a beautiful woman who designs tiles and ceramics and once designed a swimming pool for the Sultan of Brunei. Her company was once asked to repair the tile work on a mosque somewhere in the heart of the Gulf Countries. When she arrived with her son and the crates were opened, the customs officials and the guards looked heart-broken. The bits of tile looked like something had broken.

"*Khallas*," they said.

It is an Arabic word for "broken".

In Mumbai, we use it as a word for "finished" and, therefore, for "dead".

Marathi has a lot of Arabic in it, my friend the Marathi litterateur and translator, Shanta Gokhale, reminds me.

~

As I write this, I have just finished translating a Marathi book, an autobiography called *Mi Mithachi Bahuli* by Vandana Mishra. She was born Sushila Lotlikar, a Brahmin girl from the Konkan coast of Maharashtra, so close to Goa as did not make any difference. When her mother was widowed, she became a nurse. Then someone threw acid on her mother's back and she had to stop working. Her daughter became an actor and starred in Gujarati plays. Then she quit the Gujarati company and joined a Marwari theatre group and starred in *Ramu Chanana*, a great hit of its time. At the height of her success, she got married to a Champaneri Brahmin called Mishra and retired. Watch out for *The Salt Doll*.

~

"I'm caste-blind that way," says a young woman to me.

I tell Pradnya Daya Pawar, the poet and columnist, this.

"You can afford to be caste-blind if you are at the top. At the bottom, it's a luxury," she says. Her voice is remarkably free of bitterness.

~

One of my best friends is a Hindu Brahmin South Indian who learned Bharatnatyam when she was young and speaks English with a cut-glass accent. *Her* best friends seem to be three Roman Catholics: a Goan, a Mangalorean and a Jesuit priest. At her wedding, the people who signed as witnesses were a Parsi, a Christian and a Muslim. "This looks like the Minorities Commission," I said.

My friends seem to be Hindus, Parsis, Muslims and Christians in that order. I didn't order it that way. You don't order friendships. That's how it happens. And so I think what I am trying to say is that diversity is probably our natural state. Malcolm Gladwell in the *The Tipping Point* says that it takes us ten seconds to decide whether we like or dislike the person in front of us. Sure, in those ten seconds, you're looking for signs of Otherness: the marks of identity we love to smear on ourselves and specially on our women. But if those are removed, you'd probably go by your reptilian brain which developed a long time before we acknowledged that there was such a thing as diversity.

If you give diversity a chance, if you step out of your comfort zone, the world gets more confusing but it also gets amazingly richer.

~

I visit my mother in Ward 33, the Psychiatric Ward of the Sir JJ Hospital. You get used to a certain thread of bizarreness. Like the woman who says nothing but hangs on to the edge of your mother's bed like a limpet. A wardboy tries to get her to let go but she won't let go, and I gesture to him that it's all right.

The woman in the bed next to her asks us suddenly, "What's your caste?"

The limpet woman says, "*Yahaan to caste-baast nahin chalta. Yahaan to sab mental hai.*" (We have no caste here, no creed. Here, we are all mental.)

My mother smiles a little.

~

Pinto's equation:

Mixed culture = Interesting culture

The corollary to Pinto's equation:

Pure culture = ?

ACKNOWLEDGEMENTS

Francis Jarman, "By Way of an Introduction: Diversity and Alterity": some of the material in this essay was first published in the Introduction to *Encountering the Other*, ed. Francis Jarman (Rockville, MD: The Borgo Press, 2011).

Rakesh Sharma, "After the Election—What Next?", was originally published in abridged form in *Frontline* magazine, September 2014.

Githa Hariharan, "Making the City Hers", © Githa Hariharan, was first published in *Moving Worlds: A Journal of Transcultural Writings*, Vol. 13, No. 2, special issue on "Postcolonial Cities—South Asia", ed. Caroline Herbert (Leeds, UK & Singapore: University of Leeds & Nanyang Technological University, 2013).

Armene Modi, "Voices for the Voiceless—Transforming Women's Lives in Rural India": an earlier version of this essay appeared in the *Journal of the Federation of Zoroastrian Associations of North America* (FEZANA), Spring 2012, pp. 74–76, and we are grateful to the Editor, Dr. Dolly Dastoor, for permission to use the original material here.

R. Raj Rao, "Gay in India?", is taken from the author's weekly "Man to Man" column in the *Pune Mirror*, and the texts are reprinted by courtesy of that newspaper.

Manju Ramanan, "You, Me, and 'Hum'", was first published in *Encountering the Other*, ed. Francis Jarman. (Rockville, MD: The Borgo Press, 2011).

Meena Kandasamy, "Reverence::Nuisance" was first published on The Poetry International Web; "Mulligatawny Dreams" is from *Kavya Bharati* (Madurai); and "One-Eyed" first appeared in *Ms. Militancy* (New Delhi: Navayanya Publishing, 2010).

Sanjukta Dasgupta, "The Way to Go" was first published in *Abuse and Other Short Stories* (Kolkata: Dasgupta Book Company, 2013).

Arshia Sattar, "Diversity within the Valmiki Ramayana": some of the material in this essay originally appeared in "Three Cities, Three Dharmas" in the author's *Lost Loves: Exploring Rama's Anguish* (New Delhi: Penguin, 2011).

M.H. Zaffar, "Religious Fundamentalism and Secularism: With Special Reference to Islam": an earlier version was originally published in the *Journal for Peace Studies*, Volume 13, Issue 3, July-September 2006, pp. 3-9.

Gayatri Pagdi, "The Visit": earlier versions appeared in *Can We Live Together?*, published by the Centre for Communication and Development Studies (CCDS), Pune, and in the author's *Walking with Chris* (Brentwood, Essex, UK: Chipmunkapublishing, 2008).

Arundhathi Subramanian, "Where I Live" and "To the Welsh Critic Who Doesn't Find Me Identifiably Indian" are from *Where I Live: New and Selected Poems* (Hexham, Northumberland, UK: Bloodaxe, 2009); "The City and I" is from *When God Is a Traveller* (Bloodaxe, 2014).

Jerry Pinto, "The Shared Space of Hollywood": a version of this essay first appeared in a publication for Open Space, the youth outreach programme of the Centre for Communication and Development Studies, Pune.

Works Cited

Abraham, Susan. "Steal or I'll Call You a Thief: 'Criminal' Tribes of India." In: *Economic and Political Weekly*, July 3rd, 1999, 1751–53.

Baburnama (Memoirs of Babur). Transl. by Annette Susannah Beveridge (1921). Delhi: Low Price Publications, 1989.

Bhatnagar, R.S. "Hermeneutics of Religious Text." In: *The Journal of Religious Studies*, Autumn, 1992, 88–97.

Bhattacharya, Chandrima S. "Son Shows Shah Rukh Ganpati Allah—*Amar Akbar Antony* in Real Life." In: *The Telegraph*, August 14th, 2003. Website, <http://www.telegraphindia.com/1030814/asp/nation/story_2263777.asp>

Biswas, Soutik. "Why India has a 'sliver of time' to seize its chances." In: *BBC News*, March 15th, 2016. Website,
< http://www.bbc.com/news/world-asia-india-35800452>

Budhan Theatre: The Official Budhan Theatre Website,
<http://budhantheatre.org/blog/page/2/>

Bumiller, Elisabeth. *May You Be the Mother of a Hundred Sons: A Journey among the Women of India* (1990). New York: Ballantine, 1991.

Buzurg Tehrani, Shaykh Aga. "An Outline of the History of Restriction on Ijtihad" (1980–81). Transl. by Mujahid Husayn. In: *Al-Tawhid*, volume XI, January–June, 1994. Website,
<http://www.al-islam.org/al-tawhid/general-al-tawhid/outline-history-restriction-ijtihad-shaykh-aga-buzurg-tehrani/outline>

Chaudhuri, Nirad C. "The Finest Story about India—in English." In: *Encounter*, VIII, April 1957, 47–53.

———. *The Continent of Circe: Being an Essay on the Peoples of India* (1965). Bombay: Jaico, 1966.

Chhara, Daxin & Roxy **Gagdekar**. Email to the author, December 27th, 2008.

Clayton, Nick. "Google and beyond: The new Silicon Valley kingpins." In: *BBC Capital*, September 10th, 2015. Website, <http://www.bbc.com/capital/story/20150909-google-and-beyond-the-new-silicon-valley-kingpins>

Dandekar, Ajay. "A Hegemony of Silence: The Case of India's Denotified Tribes." In: *Counter-Hegemony and the Postcolonial "Other"*. Ed. Michael Hayes / Thomas Acton. Newcastle-upon-Tyne: Cambridge Scholars Press, 2006, 14–27.

Das, Gurcharan. "Porn, prudes and the parampara of optimism." In: *Sunday Times of India*, August 8th, 2015, 12. Also online, <http://gurcharandas.blogspot.de/2015/08/porn-prudes-and-parampara-of-optimism.html>

Daws, Gavan. *Prisoners of the Japanese: POWs of World War II in the Pacific*. New York: William Morrow, 1994.

Demosthenes. *Demosthenes I: Olythiacs, Philippics, Minor Public Speech, Speech against Leptines, I–XVII, XX*. Transl. by J.H. Vince. Cambridge, MA: Harvard University Press, 1930.

Devi, Mahasweta. "Born 1871—India's Denotified Tribes." In: *Budhan*, February–March, 1999. Baroda: Bhasha Research and Publication Center, 1999, 9-13.

Devy, Ganesh. "The Branded Tribes of India." In: *PUCL Bulletin*, 9, 1998. Delhi: People's Union for Civil Liberties.

———. "Giving Adivasis a Voice." In: *InfoChange India News & Features*, October 2008. Website, <http://infochangeindia.org/Agenda/Against-exclusion/Giving-adivasis-a-voice.html>

Doherty, Paul. *The Death of Alexander the Great: What—or Who—Really Killed the Young Conqueror of the Known World?* New York: Carroll & Graf, 2004.

Dostoyevsky, Fyodor. *The Brothers Karamazov* (1880). Transl. by Constance Garnett. New York: The Lowell Press, 1955.

D'Souza, Dilip. "De-Notified Tribes: Still Criminal?" In: *Economic and Political Weekly*, December 18th–24th, 1999, 3576–78.

Dutt, Nabanita. "Paradhis of India: A Tribe of Hereditary Criminals." In: *Trickster's Way*, 2, 3, July 15th, 2003. Website, <http://digitalcommons.trinity.edu/cgi/viewcontent.cgi?article=1065&context=trickstersway>

Fernando, Leonard & G. **Gispert-Sauch**. *Two Thousand Years of Faith: Christianity in India*. New Delhi: Penguin, 2004.

Francis, T. Dayanandan (Ed.). *The Christian Bhakti of A.J. Appasamy (A Collection of His Writings)*. Madras: Christian Literature Society, 1992.

Fuentes, Carlos. *The Buried Mirror: Reflections on Spain and the New World*. Boston & New York: Houghton Mifflin, 1992.

[**Gaekwad**, Laxman.] "Uchalya: The Caste of the Criminals." Excerpts from Gaekwad's novel (1988) transl. by Vikas Kamat. In: *kamat's potpourri*, Website, < http://www.kamat.com/econtent/reviews/books/uchalya.htm>

N.B. A full translation (*The Branded*), by P.A. Kolharkar, was published by Sahitya Akademi (New Delhi) in 1999.

Gascoigne, Bamber. *The Great Moghuls* (1971). New Delhi: Time Books International, 1987.

Graf, Peter. "Encountering the Other as Discovering Oneself." In: *Encountering the Other*. Ed. Francis Jarman. Rockville, MD: The Borgo Press, 2011, 17–31.

Gray, John. *Men Are from Mars, Women Are from Venus: A Practical Guide for Improving Communication and Getting What You Want in Your Relationships* (1992). New York: HarperCollins, 1993.

Grove, Trevor. "When a Prayer Can Help." In: *Observer Travel Extra: India*, September 21st, 1986, 5–6.

Guha, Ramachandra. *Savaging the Civilized: Verrier Elwin, His Tribals, and India*. Chicago: University of Chicago Press; 1999.

———. "Verdicts on Nehru: The Rise and Fall of a Reputation." In: *Patriots and Partisans*. New Delhi: Allen Lane, 2012, 123–48. (The essay is an expanded version of a talk first given in 2005.)

"Hindu Upsurge, The: The Road to Ayodhya." In: *The Economist*, February 6th, 1993, 21–22, 24.

Hobbes, Thomas. *Leviathan, or, The Matter, Forme, and Power of a Common-wealth, Ecclesiasticall and Civill* (1651). Cambridge: Cambridge University Press, 1996.

Hofstede, Geert & Gert Jan **Hofstede**. *Cultures and Organizations: Software of the Mind* (1991). Second edition. New York: McGraw-Hill, 2005.

ICMR (IBS Center for Management Research). "Case Study: The 'Incredible India' Campaign: Marketing India to the World." Website, <http://www.icmrindia.org/casestudies/catalogue/Marketing/The%20 %27Incredible%20India%27%20Campaign%20-%20Marketing%20 Case.htm>

Inglehart, Ronald. *Modernization and Postmodernization: Cultural, Economic and Political Change in 43 Societies*. Princeton, NJ: Princeton University Press, 1997.

Irving, John. *A Son of the Circus* (1994). New York: Ballantine, 1997.

Jarman, Francis. *A Star Fell: A Play* (1998). Third, U.S. edition. Rockville, MD: The Borgo Press, 2009.

———. "*Sat–*: From Exotic Custom to Relativist Controversy" (2002). Reprinted as "Burning Women" in: F. Jarman. *White Skin, Dark Skin, Power, Dream: Essays on Literature and Culture*. Holicong, PA: The Borgo Press, 2005, 95–121.

———. "Azimullah Khan—A Reappraisal of One of the Major Figures of the Revolt of 1857." In: *South Asia*, XXXI, 3, 2008, 419–49.

Khawaja, Jamal. *Quest for Islam: A Philosopher's Approach.* Bombay: Allied Publishers, 1977.

Khilnani, Sunil. *Incarnations: India in 50 Lives.* Gurgaon: Allen Lane, 2016.

Kipling, Rudyard. "Her Majesty's Servants." In: *The Jungle Book* (1894). London: Pan Books / Macmillan, 1975, 163–79.

———. *Kim* (1901). Ed. Edward W. Said. Harmondsworth, Middx.: Penguin, 1987.

Legenhausen, Muhammad. "Islam and Religious Pluralism." In: *Al-Tawhid*, Vol. XIV, Fall, 1997. Website,
<http://www.al-islam.org/al-tawhid/vol14-n3/islam-and-religious-pluralism-dr-muhammad-legenhausen>

Linton, Ralph. *The Study of Man: An Introduction.* New York: Appleton-Century-Crofts, 1936.

Luttrell, Anthony. "The Crusade in the Fourteenth Century." In: *Europe in the Late Middle Ages*. Ed. John Hale / Roger Highfield / Beryl Smalley. London: Faber & Faber, 1965, 122–54.

Mehta, Ved. *Portrait of India* (1970). Harmondsworth, Middx.: Penguin, 1973.

Michael, S.M., SVD (2009). "Cultural Diversity and Inculturation in India." In: *Sedos Bulletin*, Vol. 42, No. 3/4, March–April, 2010, 77–84. Website,
<http://www.sedosmission.org/web/en/mission-articles/doc_view/1764-cultural-diversity-and-inculturation in india>

Mosse, David. "The Politics of Religious Synthesis: Roman Catholicism and Hindu Village Society in Tamil Nadu, India." In: *Syncretism/Anti-Syncretism: The Politics of Religious Synthesis.* Eds. Charles Stewart / Rosalind Shaw. New York: Routledge, 1994, 85–107.

Mukhia, Harbans. *The Mughals of India.* Oxford: Blackwell, 2004.

Mukhopadhyay, Nilanjan. *Narendra Modi: The Man, the Times.* Chennai: Tranquebar, 2013.

Mukt-Saad (Call of the Unbound). An interdisciplinary bilingual journal focused on the Nomadic and the Denotified Communities of India. Website, < http://www.indianfolklore.org/journals/index.php/mukt>

Naqvi, Saba. *In Good Faith: A Journey in Search of an Unknown India.* New Delhi: RainLight Rupa, 2012,

"Oscars not ultimate recognition, says Amitabh Bachchan." In: *The Times of India*, January 23rd, 2009. Website, <http://timesofindia.indiatimes.com/india/Oscars-not-ultimate-recognition-says-Amitabh-Bachchan/articleshow/4022389.cms>

Pagdi, Gayatri. *Walking with Chris.* Brentwood, Essex (UK): Chipmukapublishing, 2008.

Pawar, Bhagyashri. "Will Kerala Tourism Be Affected if God's Own Country Turns into a Dog's Hell?" In: *itripto BETA*, July 17th, 2015. Website, <http://travel.india.com/articles/will-kerala-tourism-affected-gods-country-turns-dogs-hell/>

Pigott-Smith, Tim. *Out of India* (1986). Second edition. London: Duckworth, 1997.

Plato. *Great Dialogues of Plato*. Transl. by W.H.D. Rouse. New York: Mentor, 1956.

Pradhan, Bharathi S. *Colas, Cars & Communal Harmony: A Doff to Bollywood's Secular Colours.* Mumbai: India Book Distributors, 2003.

Raj, Selva J. "Dialogue 'on the Ground': The Complicated Identities and the Complex Negotiations of Catholics and Hindus in South India." In: *Journal of Hindu–Christian Studies,* Vol. 17, 2004, 33–34. Website, <http://dx.doi.org/10.7825/2164-6279.1316>

Ramanan, Manju. "We Are Not Thieves." In: *Femina Special Issue,* December 20th, 2006, 172–82.

Ramanujan, A.K. "Three Hundred Ramayaṇas: Five Examples and Three Thoughts on Translation." In: *Many Ramayanas: The Diversity of a Narrative Tradition in South Asia.* Ed. Paula Richman. Berkeley & Los Angeles, CA: University of California Press, 1991.

Ransford, Oliver. *The Slave Trade*. London: John Murray, 1971.

Richman, Paula (Ed.). *Many Ramayanas: The Diversity of a Narrative Tradition in South Asia*. Berkeley & Los Angeles, CA: University of California Press, 1991.

———. (Ed.). *Questioning Ramayanas: A South Asian Tradition.* Oxford: Oxford University Press, 2000.

———. (Ed.). *Ramayana Stories in Modern South India: An Anthology*. Bloomington, IN: Indiana University Press, 2008.

Rousseau, Jean-Jacques. *Eloisa, or, A Series of Original Letters* [*La Nouvelle Héloïse*, 1761]. English translation in three volumes. Volume two. London: John Harding *et al.*: 1810.

Rushdie, Salman. "The Half-Woman God." In: *AIDS Sutra: Untold Stories from India*. Ed. Negar Akhavi. London: Vintage Books, 2008, 109–17.

Sattar, Arshia. *Lost Loves: Exploring Rama's Anguish*. New Delhi: Penguin, 2011.

Snowden, Frank M. *Blacks in Antiquity: Ethiopians in the Greco-Roman Experience*. Cambridge, MA: Harvard University Press, 1970.

Solanas, Valerie. *SCUM Manifesto* (1967). New York: Olympia Press, 1968.

Sreekantan Nair, C.N. & Sarah Joseph. *Retelling the Ramayana: Voices from Kerala*. Transl. by Vasanthi Sankaranarayanan. New Delhi: Oxford University Press, 2005.

Summerfield, Ellen & Sandra **Lee**. *Seeing the Big Picture: A Cinematic Approach to Understanding Cultures in America*. Ann Arbor, MI: University of Michigan Press, 2006.

Sumption, Jonathan. *The Albigensian Crusade* (1978). Paperback edition. London: Faber & Faber, 1999.

Suraiya, Jug. "Times of Change." In: *The Times of India*, April 24th, 2013, 2.

Swift, Jonathan. *Gulliver's Travels* [*Travels into Several Remote Nations of the World. In Four Parts. By Lemuel Gulliver, First a Surgeon, and then a Captain of Several Ships*] (1726). Ware, Herts.: Wordsworth, 1992.

Tannen, Deborah. *Gender and Discourse*. Oxford: Oxford University Press, 1994.

Tannenbaum, Frank. *Slave and Citizen: The Negro in the Americas*. New York: Vintage Books, 1946.

Tharoor, Shashi. "Left Us Reminding He Had More to Say." In: *The New Indian Express*, July 29th, 2015, 10. Also online, <http://www.newindianexpress.com/columns/Left-Us-Reminding-He-Had-More-to-Say/2015/07/29/article2945794.ece>

Todorov, Tzvetan. *The Conquest of America: The Question of the Other* [*La Conquête de l'Amérique*, 1982]. Transl. by Richard Howard. New York: Harper & Row, 1985.

"Unity in diversity is strength of our nation"—PM Modi. In: *The Times of India*, January 28th, 2015. Website,

<http://timesofindia.indiatimes.com/india/Unity-in-diversity-is-strength-of-our-nation-PM-Modi/articleshow/46040370.cms>

Us Salam, Ziya. "An Iron Curtain on the Freedom of Thought." In: *The Hindu*, August 4th, 2015, 11. Also online, <http://www.thehindu.com/opinion/op-ed/an-iron-curtain-on-the-freedom-of-thought/article7496187.ece>

Valiyakunnel, Fr. Prince, OFMCap (2013). "From Inculturation to Interculturation in Formation." Website, <http://www.ofmconv.net/docs/sgf-biblioteca/incult/incult-02.pdf>

Valmiki. *The Ramayana*. Transl. by Arshia Sattar. London: Viking Allen Lane, 1996.

Vanita, Ruth & Saleem **Kidwai** (Eds.). *Same-Sex Love in India: Readings from Literature and History*. New York: St. Martin's Press, 2000.

"We Are Natural Allies: Exclusive Interview with Narendra Modi." In: *Time*, Vol. 185, No. 18, May 18th, 2015. Website, <http://time.com/3849494/narendra-modi-india/>

Westermann, William L. *The Slave Systems of Greek and Roman Antiquity*. Philadelphia, PA: The American Philosophical Society, 1955.

Winter, Keith John. *Shananditti: The Last of the Beothuks*. North Vancouver: J.J. Douglas, 1975.

Yoeu Ali, Anida. "Performance artist's 'Buddhist bug' questions differences." In: *BBC News*, December 12th, 2014. Website, <http://www.bbc.com/news/world-asia-30521845>

Zachary, G. Pascal. *The Diversity Advantage: Multicultural Identity in the New World Economy*. Boulder, CO: Westview Press, 2003.

Zimmern, Alfred. *The Greek Commonwealth: Politics and Economics in Fifth-century Athens* (1911). Fifth edition. Oxford: Oxford University Press, 1931.